CW01664650

The Black Country Dialect

a modern linguistic analysis

by

Ed Conduit

B.Sc., M.Sc., M.A., Dip.Clin. Psych.

2007

0 000 001 823 86

The Black Country Dialect

a modern linguistic analysis

by

Ed Conduit

ISBN
978-0-9554877-0-5

10-digit ISBN
0-9554877-0-6

Published by

Laghamon Publishing
P.O.Box 4137, Stourbridge,
West Midlands, DY7-6WZ

Contact details

Laghamon@yahoo.co.uk
Telephone 07976-646291

Printed by

Waterloo Design & Print plc, Halesowen

Disclaimer: these findings are based on limited research. Input from readers is welcome.

Front cover: Old English place names on the East side of River Severn.
Names are at various later Anglo Saxon times, are not meant to show
the relative importance of settlements or to be contemporaneous

The Black Country Dialect

Contents

1
Is Black Country Dialect grammatical?

The "Black Country" is currently taken to mean four boroughs in the West Midlands. Local people tend to think the word should be used more narrowly, to mean the former steel towns such as Darlaston, Dudley, and Cradley. Visitors from far afield may think of these towns as not very different from Birmingham. But these visitors and "Brummies" would both puzzle over phrases such as the following:

1. Tek the 'onds-free away frum yer fairse ter spake in towun"
("Move the hands-free kit further from your mouth before speaking in town")

2. Ah sid 'ern wuz wuss than yowern
("I could see that hers was worse than yours")

3. Our babby wuz took bad in the night 'n day go ter skewul
("Our child was taken ill last night and did not go to school")

4. Get shut o' the that 'wammel, cus ee's doolally. Kep the pup. It's a boster"
("Dispose of that animal, it's mad. Keep the pup, it's excellent".
Advice to a dog breeder)

These phrases are clearly a long way from standard English. Are they simply "bad grammar"? To answer that needs a modern understanding of grammar. Grammar for many centuries meant the structures needed to learn Latin, and perhaps Greek. Schoolboys and novice monks learnt that Latin verbs have conjugations, including future, perfect, future perfect, pluperfect and so on. As Latin was a prestigious language of the church, it was assumed that English had the same structures, perhaps hidden in some way. Most linguists now think this is wrong. It is unscientific to try to write a grammar for one language by comparing it with a high-prestige language. A descriptive grammar of English finds that it does not really have a future tense. Although we can say "I will go tomorrow", the "will" is really an aspect of the present, along with several other verbs like "can" and "might".

So if every dialect has its grammar, is there such a thing as "good grammar"? It is obviously useful to have a standard English. Without it builders would misunderstand architects, pilots would misunderstand air traffic controllers, and patients would misunderstand doctors more than they currently do. So it is important that people who have to communicate by writing understand, for example, the different ways apostrophe s is used in English. Most people mix up "the dog's dinner", "the dogs' competition", and "the dog's red". A prescriptive grammar rule is needed to make these distinctions. But this is about having shared conventions, rather than preserving some "pure" form of the language. Teachers used to struggle to persuade pupils to say "to whom" rather than "who to", but have now mostly given up. "Whom" is falling into disuse in English. Is there is a reason to keep fighting that lost battle? Having a standard English also means that we continue with many out-of-date and odd rules, particularly an obsolete spelling. When Caxton described the tool used by farmers he called it a "plogh" in his Kentish dialect, pronouncing it to rhyme with Scottish "loch". Unfortunately we are now stuck with the spelling "plough", which is nothing like the modern "plow". The sound that used to be pronounced and written "ough" may now be pronounced "ow", "off" or "or". A rational spelling would follow pronunciation, but the disruption of changing it would be very great.

Modern linguists now think of "grammar" as something people have in their brain. They were not taught it, and indeed do not know what its rules are. The linguist's task is to find out what these unspoken rules are, by asking native speakers which sentences sound right, and which break the rule. Chapters 6 to 8 of this book attempt to do this for phonetics, word endings, and meter.

A dialect is more than an accent, as it has syntax and word ending differences from the high language as well as accent, but is not a separate language. Brummie might thus better be described as an accent rather than a dialect. Scots is now a dialect of English, but was a separate language in 1600. Prestige is an important feature of any dialect. English has had a standard "high" language for several centuries. The comparison of English dialects is called sociolinguistics. Surveys usually find that some dialects are seen as more educated and influential than others. Speakers with Edinburgh accents are often seen as more knowledgeable than those with Glasgow accents. The perception of high prestige is strongly associated with education, and low prestige with heavy manual work. Belfast accents (or more accurately, the Lallands dialect) are particularly unpopular in other parts of the UK. Unpopular dialects suggest manual work, especially in the shipyards, in the nineteenth and early twentieth century. Black Country Dialect (BCD) has not been studied very much, but it has the same associations of rough manual work, and rough sports like bare-knuckle boxing and dogfights. It may be thought of as the language of steel mills, mines, and canals, and the homes of the people who worked there.

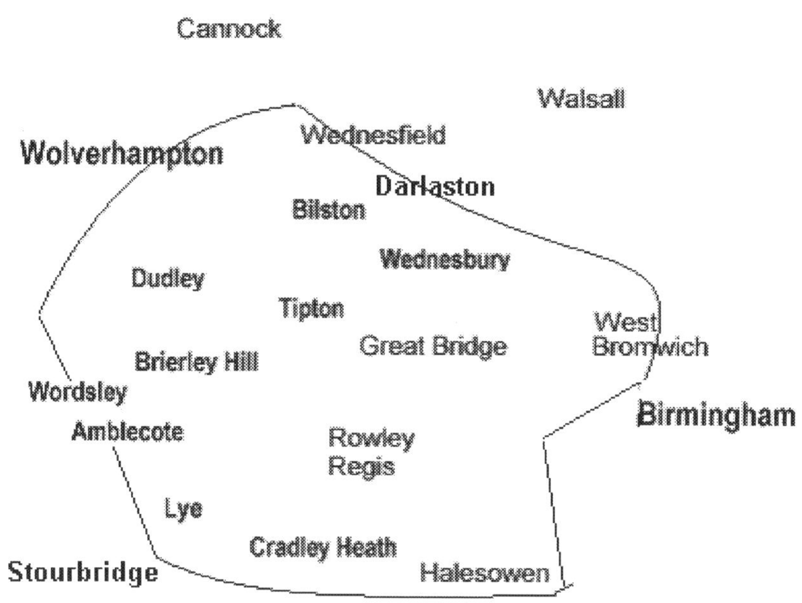

The area of the Black Country, based on former steel towns.

This is smaller than the modern use of the term, which brackets the boroughs of Sandwell, Dudley, Walsall, and Wolverhampton.

BCD has rarely been used for prestigious communications by scientists, politicians, or doctors. How would you react to the following advice from two doctors?

"Yer 'art is bostin, mate. Dow worry abaht it."

"I can reassure you that your BP is not in the hypertensive range"

You would probably be more doubtful about the first, even if the doctor came from your town. If your conversation were about the merits of beer, or your team's chances in Saturday's match, the use of dialect might be more acceptable. Would you accept this advice from the first doctor?

"The mild in 'ere is shite. Ah'll 'av bitter"
"The striker's bostin' when he teks a cross on iz yed"

The word "shite" above is both quite vulgar and quite ancient. It has the same source as "get shut on", meaning to free from unwanted attention. In Old English it was "scyttan", but this also continues prehistoric "skuttjan". This sense of vulgarity highlights the effects of words from French and German. English is originally a language of the Germanic group, but has borrowed enormously from other languages. You have already been asked to cope with some words of Greek origin, such as "syntax". Scientific language contains many such multi-syllable words, coming from Latin and Greek. Educated writing uses some of these, and a lot of loanwords from French. After the Norman conquest French was the language of a small ruling elite, and Anglo Saxon the spoken language of the majority. The Normans tried to make their manors sound attractive. Among the few French names in the West Midlands is Bewdley, which is identical with "beau lieu" ("beautiful place"). This prettification is even more obvious in the Essex village of Beaumont ("beautiful mount"), which replaced the Saxon name Fulanpettæ ("foul pit"). There may a continuing sense in modern English speakers that French is educated and cultured, and Anglo Saxon is rough and practical. There is also dislike of German because of two world wars, though this is quite recent. Hostility to France and alliance with German-speaking areas has been much more usual in most centuries. The persistence of Anglo-Saxon forms, and resistance to French will be a major theme in this book.

Black Country dialect has hardly been studied by linguists. Rare exceptions are the Ph.D. thesis of Asprey (2003), and the phonetics research by Mathisen (1999) in Sandwell. The closest serious linguistic study is of Cannock by Christopher Heath (1980). The material for this book came from a linguistics research project at Manchester University. Field work in linguistics needs native speakers who are confident about their dialect. Such people are few and far between in the Black Country. Speakers of Yorkshire dialects are likely to have a positive sense about their speech, seeing it as the language of the community, side-by-side with standard English for education. Black Country is not felt to be a language of the neighbourhood in the same way. Speakers often feel their speech is ugly, that they drop their aitches and use rough words, because they have not been properly educated. Many have experienced ridicule about their dialect.

We were therefore particularly fortunate to have George as an informant. He spent most of his life in Darlaston, and speaks proudly in the local fashion. Much of his working life was as a labourer in a steel mill. He can also speak an upper-class form of English from his time as an officer's batman, and can sing in various accents from his time as an opera singer. He gave a fluent description of how the dialect is spoken, without the need to apologise or correct it. We are also grateful to other informants, who volunteered their expertise as fluent speakers of the dialect.

How this book is organised

The four sentences above need discussion by the following specialties of linguistics. Sentence 4 introduces some unusual vocabulary. Are these different pronunciations of standard English words? If not, where do they come from? These are lexical questions, discussed in chapter two. We might ask questions about the sounds in sentence 1: does the "hands-free kit" become "onds-free" because the "a" is before a nasal sound, as in "man" and "hammer"? These are questions of phonetics, which are considered in chapter six. The "towun" in sentence 1 and the "skewel" in sentence 3 both have seem to have an extra syllable. Is that because they are at the very end? Would it be the same in "town centre" and "schoolwork"? These are questions of phonology and meter, discussed in chapter eight. Sentence 2 gives other questions: is "sid" regularly the simple past of "see", or is it just this speaker's peculiar way? What sentences can the pronouns "ern" and "yowern" be used in? What is the conjugation of the unusual verbs in sentence 3, "wuz took bad", and "day go"? These are morphological questions, about Black Country pronouns and verbs, and are discussed in chapter seven. The historical context of Modern English is needed first. Old English is described in chapter three, Early Middle English in four, and Early Modern English in five.

We shall find that Black Country is a complex, grammatical dialect with a deep history.

2
Words: where do they come from?

Although many dialect words cannot be found in standard dictionaries, they can be found in specialised dictionaries. The Oxford English Dictionary Online now has an enormous range of words, some of which are obsolete or occur only in regions. The other major reference is Joe Wright, who produced between 1898 and 1905 six volumes of English dialect words. Ted Walker in Wednesbury has collected a large list of words from the Black Country. Nearly all Walker's words can be found in one of these two sources if we look hard enough. The full list of words is in the appendix.

Other English dialects

Let us first remove a few words that are often thought to come from the West Midlands, but are actually from other languages.

bint (girl)	Arabic	**buckshee** (free, alms)	Arabic
kibosh (end)	Yiddish, perhaps	**doolally** (insane)	Marashtra, India

Most such words were brought home by returning soldiers. The Stewponey Inn was a famous landmark on the Wolverhampton to Kidderminster road. One theory of the origin of this unlikely name is that the first publican was a veteran of the peninsular war, who named it after his wife's home town, Estepona. There are other theories, including Stour + pons, and a stew-pond for fish. Returning sailors from WW2 brought other souvenirs from military service, including:

gash (waste grinder in a submarine) **sprog** (novice sailor, hence child)

A further group of words are dialect or slang, but from other English-speaking areas. Many are likely to have come with migrant workers. Some came with music hall, and a few came from Cant, the dialect of thieves. These include:

argey-bargey	Scots, 19th. C	**barney**	probably Australian
berk	rhyming slang	**dobbin**	Irish
fizzog	Yorks/ Lancs	**flummox**	probably Scots
gain (skilful)	Yorks	**gawk**	Warks, Lancs etc.
gob	possibly Irish	**guff**	possibly American
iffy	American, 20th. C	**jallop**	Scots
jammy	Kipling	**kerfuffle**	Scots
mooch	widespread, Aus	**nosh**	American, 19th. C
spondoolicks	American, 19th. C	**clock** (hit)	Australia
clobber (clothing)	possibly Cant	**flog**	possibly Cant

There are a large number of words describing drunkenness. Walker gives 36, and another 50 meaning drinking. Most of them also have the sense of having been beaten in a fight. A few are:

'alf cut	**hammered**	**sozzled**	**kalied**
smashed	**bladdered**	**pie-eyed**	**paralytic**

Vowels

Black Country has rarely been written down in modern times. When it is written, novel spellings are used to convey the distinctive effect of the dialect. Bob Bibby (2001) gives this example of a dialogue between two well-known local characters, who were given biblical names Enoch and Eli in the fashion of the nineteenth century.

Aynuk returns from his first visit to the seaside, and says to Ali,
"I si'd an iron boat sairling on the say."
"Doh be saft, Aynuk", said Ayli, "it ud sink."
"I tell yow it day sink", insisted Aynuk.
So when he gets home, in order to prove whether Aynuk was right or wrong, Ayli throws the iron bedstead into the cut. And, of course it sinks. Next day Ayli sees Aynuk and says to him:
"I thort yow told me that an iron boat day sink. Well I've chucked th'ode bedstead
in the cut and it went strairt to the bottom."
"Goo on, you fewel", says Aynuk. "Do yow know yow gorrave salt wairter?"

Most of the spellings show vowels that are different from standard English, but the words (lexical items) are the same. Vowel differences are the most significant feature of Black Country, and warrant a chapter of their own. A few of these spellings show assimilation, e.g. "gorrave" for "got to have". Many of Walker's "words" are actually pronunciation differences, and a few are differences in endings (morphological).

Core Black Country Vocabulary

Having eliminated imports from other English-speaking areas and phonetic variations, we are left with a few dozen words that are used mainly in the West Midlands. Most of these are Staffordshire or Worcestershire agricultural words. A few are Middle English words that have died out in standard English. The best-known Black Country word is "bostin", meaning excellent. It is used with "fittle", which is clearly a Midlands variant of victuals. It is not clear where "bostin" comes from. It might come the preacher Wyclif's word "worthy of boast", though Wyclif was criticising boastfulness. Bibby thinks it comes from Old English "bogan". It could mean "bursting". "Bosten" is also a carpenter's pattern.

There is a nostalgic interest in dialect words. Language is continually changing, often with technology. It is useful to ask which words are dying out as the technology disappears. The following words were read out to informants. The percentage shows how many of those informants could use the word appropriately. Meanings may be found in the appendix.

How well-known are BCD dialect words?

bibble	75%	moil	15%
bladdered	70%	monty	60%
blart	100%	muggins	100%
bostin	100%	napper	25%
bobowler	85%	nisgul	30%
chobble	55%	nincompoop	90%
clammed	92%	pleck	10%
clock (N)	55%	poke	75%
conk	35%	reisty	35%
donny	90%	riffy	80%
fittle	92%	rile	80%
fold, fod, fode	65%	sad shop	10%
gale	50%	saded, saided	10%
gammittin	75%	scuff	25%
gawby	60%	segs	25%
gawk	80%	shed	50%
get shut of	90%	spug/spujerk	15%
gleed	40%	shommox	25%
groaty	60%	skinny	80%
gob	90%	sough	20%
gubbins	15%	spottle	75%
cack/kek-handed	80%	suck	65%
hiver-hover	80%	tacky bonk	25%
ike	60%	tenter hooks	60%
kind	80%	thrape	80%
leasow, lezzer	15%	tiddler	80%
loose	88%	tundish	40%
mardy	92%	wammel	55%
maergrum	25%	wazzin	33%
maunch	85%	werrit	15%
miskin	30%	yampy	100%

It can be seen that many of the agricultural words are falling into disuse. Agriculture continued to be practised in the Black Country until well into the twentieth century. Many industrial workers kept a few pigs or sheep, so Staffordshire and Worcestershire words connected with animal husbandry persisted. Very few now keep animals other than pets, so words such as “leasow”, “pleck”, “nisgul”, “weasand”, and “spugger” are not widely known. The word “bobowler” (moth) is still known, as it used as a metaphor for a young person who stops out late. Some agricultural words survive with a generally critical sense, implying stupidity, dirtiness or other disparagements, and their original sense has been lost, e.g. “riffy”, a sheep having reeves on its skin, “blart” a lamb or calf calling.

Industrial words have also fallen into disuse. Few young adults had heard "tacky bonk", "ladegorn", or "sough". The words "fittle", "mardy", "clammed", "donny", and "cack-handed" are still widely used by young people, and would probably not be understood outside the West Midlands. The Middle English words "tundish" and "gleed" are becoming less common, probably because beer funnels and fire embers are now infrequent.

Status: Germanic vs. French

Black Country is often viewed quite negatively by outsiders. The status effect of words of French and Germanic origin can be seen in the following two statements, which say more or less the same thing:

> There'll be tea and cake in the break
> Refreshments will be available in the interval

The caff owner would expect people wanting value for money. The restaurant proprietor who used the second kind of vocabulary would expect a more refined clientele - and charge them higher prices! Black Country is a spoken dialect only, so Germanic words dominate as expected. So what about phrases and longer pieces of connected speech? In the sayings below the nouns and verbs that are of French origin are marked in italics.

Idiom	Meaning
Allus in the lezzer when yow orter be in the lairne	In the wrong place at the wrong time
Ee con dish it out but ee cor tek it	He cannot take criticism
Er's got a *voice* on 'er like a glede under a dooer	Her voice scrapes
Gie a mon a *bairsin* o broth an 'it 'im over the yed with the spewn	Give with one hand and take away with the other
'Iz fairther wo be jed so long as 'e's alive	He looks just like his father
Marry the miskin for the muck and get *pizened* with the *pizen* in it	Marry for money and regret it
Traipsing in and out like a dog at a *fair*	Restless
Rattle like a bibble in a can	Noisy
To put the beans to *bile*	Get started
Nicky nicky note, shoe the little cote, ere a nail and theer a nail, and take fast hote	Nursery rhyme about a young horse
The blartin cow soon forgets its calf	Grief is exaggerated
All round the Wrekin	Circumlocution
A nod's as good as a wink to a blind horse	I take the hint
Gud mon round a *barrel* but no cooper	A noted drinker
'Am fisted	Clumsy
'As an 'oller leg	Has a huge appetite
'Op an' a catch	Now and then
'Ow's yer father	No messing about

I cud do that afower brefuss	An easy job
I should coco	I am sceptical
If me aunt ad been a mon she'd a bin me uncle	That reasoning does not follow
I'll go to the foot of our stairs	I am surprised
It's black over Bill's (or Harry's) mother's	It looks like rain
Kick the bucket	Die
Mind 'ow yow cross the 'oss road	Take care
Put wood in th'ole	Close the door
Same to yow with knobs on!	Insulting reply
'Sling yer 'ook	Go away!
Summat the cat drug up	Bedraggled
Some 'usbands am like Bilston mines – theer's good stuff in 'em if onny yow could get'em dry, but they'm olluz soaked	Drunken husbands are like waterlogged mines

Black Country: its Germanic roots

Among the nouns and verbs in the idioms listed above, the italicised words make up only about 15%. If this list of words and idioms is representative, it means that over 80% of Black Country words are of Anglo Saxon origin, with only about 15% French, and occasional words from Norse or elsewhere. "Monty, "rile" and "mither" may be French. "Gain" is one of the rare Norse words in the dialect. This and the saying "put wood in t'ole" are probably imported from Yorkshire.

The persistence of Middle English words in Black Country is sometimes described by writers such as Bob Bibby as "Chaucerian". However, Chaucer's English was that spoken on the North Sea coast, heavily influenced by Norse. Readers may be surprised to hear Black Country described by the linguistic term "Germanic". To consider what this means, we will have to look at Old English in the next chapter.

3
Lichfield around 850

Anglo-Saxon bands started moving into England from what are now Denmark and North Germany soon after Roman power collapsed. They were warlike, and engaged the native Celts in battle. The mythological figures of Hengist and Horsa were supposed to be the first Saxons. While the Celts struck back, the general trend was for them to be pushed westwards, into Cumbria, Wales, and Cornwall. Migrant Saxons looked for new settlements, and found them in the Midlands. The front cover of this book shows many place names where they found meadows (leah) or river valleys (halh).

Old English was a Germanic language, along with Swedish, Icelandic, Friesian and Gothic. The grammar looks like modern-day German: nouns had three genders and four cases. The most influential dialect was West Saxon, especially after Alfred unified England in the war against the Danes. Most surviving literature is in West Saxon. The dialect of the Midlands and North was Mercian. There are only a few texts in Mercian, and the Vespasian Psalter is the most reliable.

Detail from Tettenhall coat of arms showing battle axes

There is little evidence of Norse settlement in the areas of Staffordshire and Worcestershire. There are Norse place names in North Staffordshire and Tamworth, but virtually none in the Black Country. The Mercians and West Saxons had a famous but costly victory over the Norse in the Battle of Tettenhall in 909. The Watling Street was the boundary for Norse rule in the period of the Danelaw, and some Danish settlers came nearly as far West as Lichfield. Standard English shows much influence from Norse, so Norse features in the dialect entered Black Country from that route.

There were other contact languages. One surprising find is a gold dinar, minted by King Offa of Mercia between 758-796 CE (CE means common era, the religiously-neutral alternative to AD). It was probably the first gold coin minted in England. On one side it says in Arabic "there is no god but Allah ...", and the other it says "Offa Rex". Some UK Muslims have concluded that Offa converted to Islam. It is much more likely that Moorish gold coins were overstamped, and neither Offa's mint master nor anyone else in Mercia could read Arabic. Friesian and other Germanic dialects were more important.

Writing was quite rare in early Anglo Saxon times, before the need to propagate the Christian gospels. Occasionally builders would cut their name on a beam, using the Norse runic script. The set of characters was called a futhorc, which uses the first six characters, rather as the word alphabet uses the first two Greek characters. The Anglo-Saxon futhorc has seven more runes than those used in Denmark in 400 CE.

The futhorc used by Anglo-Saxons was:

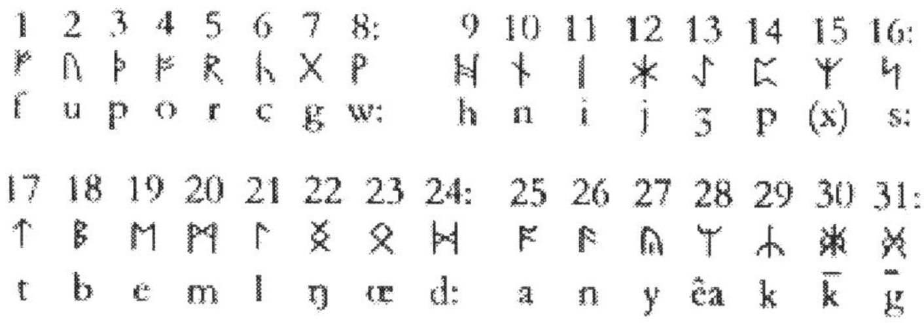

Anglo Saxon Place Names

Place names in South Staffordshire and North Worcestershire are almost entirely Anglo-Saxon. The Scandinavian professor Ekwall produced a comprehensive list of them in 1936. There are many meadows: *Segleslei* (Sedgley), and *Cradder's Lea* (Cradley), *Dudder's Lea* (Dudley, meadow of Dudder), *Hryeg Lea* (Rugeley), *Ruh Leah* (Rowley, broad and rugged land). Valleys are also common: *Willa's Halh*, *Cod's Halh, Wals Halh, Halh's Owen*. *Bramwich ham* (Birmingham) is a place where broom grew. Places associated with the persistence of worship of the god Woden are well-known: *Woden's Burg* (Wednesbury), and *Woden's Feld* (Wednesfield). *Tuns* were enclosures: *Cweningtun* (Quinton, farm of Cwena or perhaps the Queens manor). *Wulfruna's Heantown* is now Wolverhampton. *Bilsetnatum* is now Bilston, and means sharp-ridge-farmstead. The majority of the place-names on the front cover map have Anglo Saxon forms, unmodified by French.

Welsh influence is seen in only a handful of place names in Staffordshire. *Penn* and *Penkridge* are Celtic, but the second is a Welsh version of the Latin name. *Bre* (hill) in Brewood, *cnoc* (high place) in Cannock are other rare examples. Some river names were taken over from Welsh: the Severn appears to derive from the Celtic *Hafren*, while the Avon is simply the normal Welsh word for any river. There was a little-known community called the Wycchers (or Hwicce), who left us only a few place names such as *Wychbold*, and the tradition of plaiting willow wands. They may have been a mixture of Celts and Saxons.

French place names are also less common in this part of the Midlands than in most of the United Kingdom. *Beaulieu* (Bewdley) and *Beaudesert* in Cannock Chase are rare exceptions. There were few Norman manors. Haden Hill and Enville are the exceptions. Enville appears at first sight to be a French name, but is actually an assimilation of the previous Saxon name *Evenefeud*. Its manor includes Pensnett Chase, which is a French assimilation of Saxon Pensnæd, via Peninak

Mercia was the dominant kingdom for a time, particularly when Offa built his dyke against the Welsh. While the Vikings were in occupation of most of England, the surviving independent Saxons were under Alfred in the far west. He was successful against the Vikings, and because of this West Saxon became the dominant dialect. This mattered for government and law, so most surviving Old English is written in this dialect. Latin was the language for religious purposes. Most Mercians continued to speak their own dialect in their markets. So at the time of the Norman conquest the people of Staffordshire and Worcestershire spoke Mercian. They would have made themselves easily understood along the east coast and the north, and with a little more difficulty on the south coast and in Kent. They felt themselves similar to Saxons, Danes, or Friesians, but different from Britons.

Mercian and the Bible

Mercian was spoken through most of the Midlands and North and East Anglia, and was only slightly different from the Northumbrian spoken around Durham. The most substantial manuscripts in written Mercian are thought to come from the quills of monks in the diocese of Lichfield. They are sections of the Bible. Monks would take a Latin copy and write their own English translation between the lines. (This is called an interlinear gloss.) The bible has continued to be the major reason for dialect writing. A rare example of modern regional writing is found in Kate Fletcher's (1979) Old Testament in Black Country dialect. One surviving Mercian text is the Rushworth manuscripts.

The Vespasian collection of psalms (Kuhn, 1990) is the most substantial Mercian text. The Vespasian scribe tells us he came from "Harewood". Although it was at one time assumed to come from such a village in Yorkshire, and at another time from Kent, it now seems likely it came from the major religious centre at Lichfield. A feeling for Mercian can be gained from this extract from Vespasian, which can be dated to the second quarter of the 9th. Century.

> Wynsumiað gode, all eorðe; ðiowiað Dryhtne in blisse;
> ingað in gesihðe his in wynsumnisse.

Believe it or not, this is English! It is actually easier to read for a modern German than a modern English speaker. If you know some German, "eorðe" is more like "Erde" than "earth", you might guess that "Dryhtne" is another name for God, and "Wynsumiað" looks like the verb that comes from the noun "Wynsumnisse", meaning rejoicing.

Epic stories were a major apart of Anglo Saxon life. The main surviving epic is that of Beowulf. Although it was written down in England around 1000 AD, the story it tells is set in Denmark some centuries earlier. The Englishmen of this time did not see any reason to put distance between themselves and the Norse men they had fought, and the pagan symbolism is only slightly concealed by a Christian topping. The hero Beowulf is called on to fight the monster Grendel. The following extract is taken from Chapter XI, line 710.

Anglo Saxon		Modern English
Ða com of more	under misthleoþum	Then from the moorland, by misty crags,
Grendel gongan,	godes yrre bær;	with God's wrath laden, Grendel came.
mynte se manscaða	manna cynnes	The monster was minded of mankind now
sumne besyrwan	in sele þam hean.	sundry to seize in the stately house.

This is as difficult for the modern reader as the Mercian psalm. Two unfamiliar letters turn out to be quite easy: "ð" and "þ" are the voiced and unvoiced "th" sound.

Mercian Endings

The word for "name" had four different endings: it could be the subject of a verb, the direct object of a verb, the owner of another noun, or the indirect object of a verb. It was also masculine. The word for "sun" was feminine, and the word for "eye" had neuter gender. Henry Sweet wrote the grammar of West Saxon at Oxford in 1882, and it looks just like a modern German grammar. The cases of these three nouns are shown below.

	Masc		Fem		Neuter	
	Sing	Pl	Sing	Pl	Sing	Pl
Nom	nam-a	nam-an	sunn-e	sunn-an	ēag-e	ēag-an
Acc	nam-an	nam-an	sunn-an	sunn-an	ēag-an	ēag-an
Gen	nam-an	nam-ena	sunn-an	sunn-ena	ēag-an	ēag-ena
Dat	nam-an	nam-um	sunn-an	sunn-um	ēag-an	ēag-um

Verbs also had more endings than modern English. Nowadays one form (the stem) is used for everything, except the "he/ she" form. (I have, you have, he has, we have, they have). There was also a "thou" form. This is rarely used now, but we can still understand its sense. Around 1000 AD there were two distinct forms of the verb to be: "wesan" and "beon". There was still a difference between the singular and plural form, though the plural forms were the same whether the speaker meant "we", "ye", or "they". The forms of the verbs are shown below. Not only do they look like German, they also look a little like Black Country.

	modern	wesan	beon
1S	I am	eam	beo
2S	you are	eart	bist
3SM	he is	is	bith
3SF	she is	is	bith
1PL	we are	sind	beon
2PL	you are	sind	beon
3PL	they are	sind	beon

How different were the dialects of English? Anglo Saxons from all over England would have understood each other fairly well. In the table above Mercian and Northumbrian had ic (e)am for "I am", while West Saxon had "eom" in the first person. Mercian and West Saxon differed mainly in the vowel sounds. In many situations Mercian had "o" where West Saxon had "a". Another difference was that Mercian had "e" where West Saxon had a diphthong "ea", as in the following examples:

MODERN	MERCIAN	WEST SAXON
all	all	eall
sold (pp.)	sald	seald
wall	wall	weall

West Saxon under Alfred came to exercise a dominating effect on Old English, but this disappeared after 1066. The varieties of Middle English are the subject to the next chapter.

4
The Severn Valley 1200-1400

Saxon, French, Norse

Middle English differs from Old English mainly through the influence of French, some influence of Norse, and by developing an isolating grammar. To describe English as an isolating language is to say that it uses separate words, especially prepositions, rather than changing the ending of words.

The replacement of West Saxon by Norman French as the official or "high" language was the main reason for change. Most people did not speak French, and continued to speak local dialects of English. As these were rarely written, they tended to diverge. Educated people were trilingual: they used French for law and culture, Latin for religion, and English for many practical issues.

Many words from French were borrowed by English speakers. Sometimes they expanded the vocabulary. A well-known example is the way English acquired words for cooked meat different from those used for the animals they came from, e.g. mutton, pork, beef, venison. Sometimes Germanic and French words were used side by side, with more or less the same meaning. This is most obvious in legal phrases, e.g. "goods and chattels", to allow English speakers to follow court proceedings. Rarely a French word replaced a Germanic one.

Norse continued to have big effects on English while French was the high language of England. A major example is replacement of *them* for *hem.* The effect of Norse is harder to trace, as there is a lack of documents. Danish had been spoken all along the coast of the North Sea, and Norwegian in what is now Cumbria. The changes were occurring long after the collapse of the Danelaw. It is likely that Danish speakers gradually abandoned their language in favour of English, but brought some words with them. This is similar to what happened when speakers of Scots adopted London English. A child can acquire easily the endings (inflections) of nouns in his parents' language. It takes an adult learning it as second language much longer. English may have been spoken as a second language by people who were giving up Danish. Difficulty in mastering inflections may have been a reason for giving them up in favour of prepositions. The large expansion of London came by immigration of smiths and merchants from East Anglia.

Wyclif's preachers spread an English version of the gospels from their base in Lutterworth. Some Wyclif phrases continue in Midlands English. Standard English emerged rather forcefully around 1420, mainly for the publication of laws. Chancery Standard English is the name given to it. Chaucer's poetry was a major source of standard English. In the period 1066 to 1425 Early Middle English persisted in various dialects. As there was no "high" version, there was little pressure for standardisation. Wyclif's insistence on teaching the gospels in English was a major boost for the language, though it cost him dear: his skeleton was hung after his death, as he was deemed a heretic.

The Great Vowel Shift

The change to an isolating language took English further away from its cousins. Many features that still exist in modern German disappeared. The four noun cases largely merged. The dative case was replaced by prepositions such as "to" and "for". Modern nouns now have only one case, but retain an *–s* ending to show when something is owned. Modern pronouns retain three cases, e.g. "he/ him/ his". The three genders were abandoned, so that most nouns have common gender unless they have obvious biological gender. Other Germanic languages such as Dutch also reduced their genders, though not as much as English.

The Great Vowel Shift in later Middle English is particularly interesting. All the vowels of standard English changed between the time of Chaucer and that of Shakespeare. Chaucer lived in what would have sounded like a *hoos*, with his *weef*, and *hay* would romance *heer* with a bottle of *weena*, drunk by the light of the *moan*. Shakespeare would have pronounced them in more or less the modern way, as *house*, *wife*, *he*, *her*, *wine*, and *moon.*

To understand the Great Vowel Shift, a little phonetics is needed. Vowels differ mainly in the position of the tongue. All vowels involve voicing with vocal cords, but the sound is shaped by the size of the resonating space made in the mouth. Think of the mouth as like the box on a violin, cello or double bass. The small noise made by the strings is amplified by the resonant cavity; a small cavity makes a high note, a big one makes a low note.

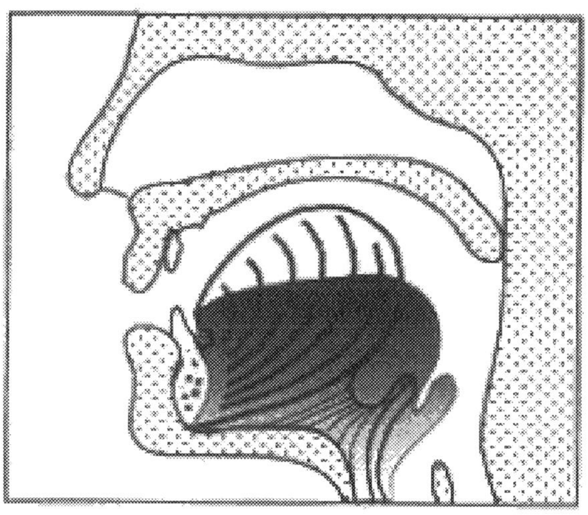

Tongue position for "ee"

When the tongue is high up near the teeth at the front, we hear an *ee* sound, as in "teeth".

When the tongue is in the postion shown by ark shading, we hear an "aa" or "ŏ"

Middle English (c.1100 – 1450)		Early Modern English (c. 1450-1600)	
iː	→	ei	(closest → diphthong)
eː	→	iː	
ɛː	→	eː	
aː	→	ɛː	
ɔː	→	oː	
oː	→	uː	
uː	→	ou	(closest → diphthong)

This rather complicated pattern may be summarized by the general rule that after the GVS most vowels became "one step closer", and the previously closest became diphthongs. The position of the tongue is conventionally described as close (to the roof of the mouth), mid-close, mid-open, or fully open. It is unclear why the GVS happened. To keep words separate, all vowels had to move at the same time, although some words merged in their sound. "Meet" and "meat" sounded different before the GVS but the same after it. The UCL linguist John Wells argues that these shifts have affected all dialects of English, at least in respect of front vowels. This may be doubted, as we shall see later.

Who lived in the Black Country?

Staffordshire was a prosperous area in Mercian times, particularly along the Trent valley. In the Early English period South Staffordshire and North Worcestershire were of relatively low value. We can infer this from the Domesday book, which gives the tax liability or 'hidages' of parishes. Extracts of maps for South Staffordshire and West Warwickshire are shown below. The implication is that William the conqueror's troops wreaked destruction following Saxon revolts, though there is little direct evidence of this. A parish in the North East has a productive 25.5, and there is a large hidage of 18 at Penkridge. These compare unfavourably with 39.5 for Stratford-on-Avon. Dudley does not appear to generate much tax, and Wolverhampton rated only 4.5. The most southerly parish of Staffordshire warrants a relatively productive 12 hides; this appears to include the valley of the Stour, and Rowley Regis.

Map of Domesday hidages (redrawn from Gelling, 1992)

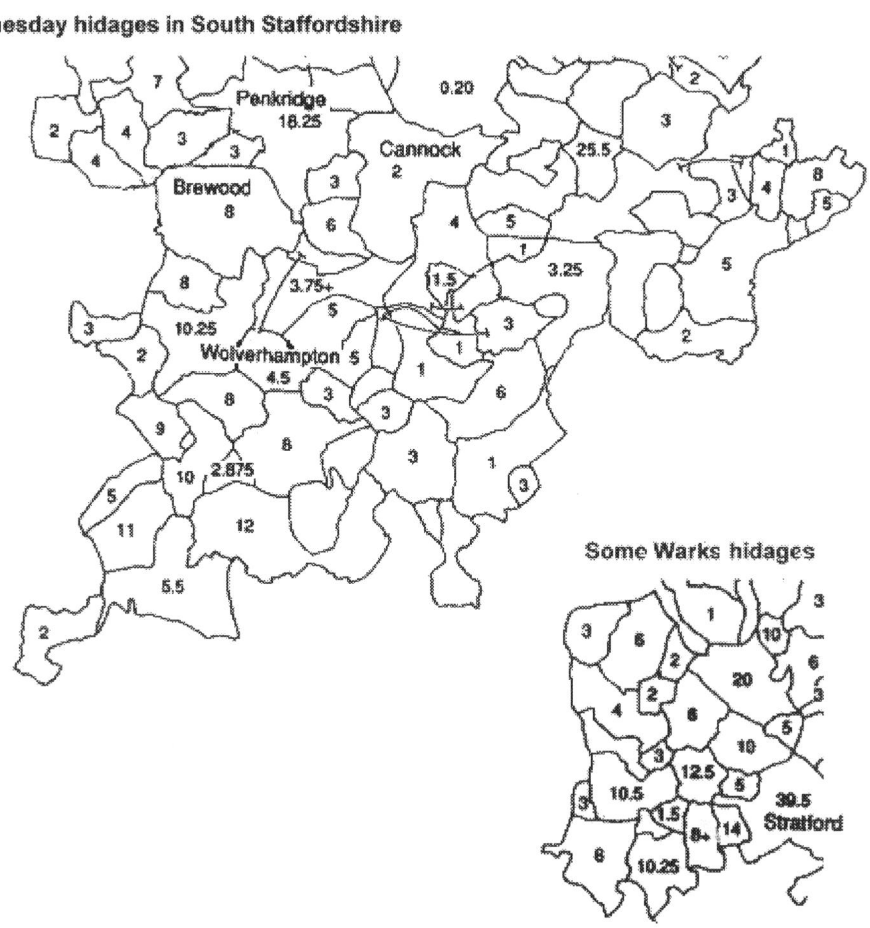

We may assume, without much documentary evidence, that there were few people in Black Country before about 1400. There were perhaps only 15,000 people in the whole of Staffordshire in 1327. Most of these were in the larger population centres, in the far east of the county on the River Trent at Burton and Tamworth. The higher ground away from rivers might have supported a few hundred people. The "leahs" at Dudley and Sedgley might have been only summer pastures, or scattered farmsteads. Dudley always had a garrison population, after its seizure by Ansculf of Picquiny from the Earl of Mercia, and Halesowen had a population around its Abbey. However, it may be doubted whether these hamlets were large enough to be a speech community. The population is presumed to have expanded only after iron became important, and migrants moved from the counties along the Severn valley. This argues that the speech community for what is now Black Country was then spoken widely along the Severn.

Midlands English

Midlands English during this period is known from only a few texts. The principal ones are the Ancrene Wisse, Gawain and the Green Knight, Laghamon's Brut, and Piers Plowman.

All use alliterative verse. We now experience it in headlines like "saucy stripper in sex romp", such as might be found in tabloid newspapers. The word alliteration means repetition of an initial sound. However, it also says something about metrical stress. The following are the precise requirements for alliterative verse. Each line is divided into two half lines, with a definite break in the middle. One consonant at the beginning of a stressed syllable is used repeatedly in each pair of half-lines. There must be two stressed and two unstressed syllables. Alliteration is similar in Old Saxon, Old Icelandic, and Old High German, and quite unlike poetic writing in Middle French.

The Ancrene Wisse (or Ancrene Riwle) is a book of guidance to female hermits, then known as anchorites. It is thought to have been written in Worcestershire, perhaps around 1215. The Wisse is easier to read if you know some modern German or Dutch. It is remarkable that a century and half after the Norman conquest his passage shows virtually no evidence of French.

Part of the reason the extract below is hard to read is that there are several letters that are no longer used. The letters þ and ð (called unvoiced and voiced dental fricatives by phoneticians) are now both written "th". The letter "3" is more awkward, as the sound no longer exists in English. We can still make the sound, by saying the modern Scots sound in "Auchtermuchtie".

Worcestershire Middle English, 1215	Modern English
Nu easki 3e hwet riwle 3e ancren schulen halden. 3e schulen alles weis, wið alle mihte ant strengðe, wel witen þe inre, ant te uttre for hire sake. Þe inre is eauer ilich, þe uttre is mislich; for euch schal halden þe uttre efter þet ha mei best wið hire serui þe inre.	Now you ask what rule you anchoresses should observe. You should in every way, with all your might, scrupulously observe the inner rule, and the outer for the sake of the inner. The inner rule is always the same, the outer varies; because everyone should observe the outer rule in the way that helps her best to follow the inner.

Another major writing from the Midlands is Gawain and the Green Knight. JRR Tolkien, who grew up in Moseley, published a book on Gawain and the Green Knight (Tolkien and Gordon, 1967) before writing the Lord of the Rings. This is a story of temptation and honourable resistance. The author is unknown, but he (or she) is also thought to have written the Pearl, and some other works. They are in a dialect characterised as being West Midland, though this may be Cheshire or Lancashire. A few other texts exist in early West Midlands. These include a prose psalter, and William and the Werwolf in the 1300s. A dictionary of Middle English was published by Stratmann (1974).

Lower Arley in 1205

Laghamon's Brut is a history of the English people, written about 1205. Laghamon was a priest whose church was on the west bank of the Severn, opposite modern Stourport. The village is identified in the verse below as Earnley, but is also known as Areley Kings, to distinguish it from Upper Arley. The surname now appears in several street names in Areley Kings as Layamon. However, it seems more likely his name was pronounced with the obsolete "gh" sound. The author tells us his plan right at the beginning:

Worcs Middle English (1205)

A prest was in londe. Laweman was hote.
he was Leucais sone. lef him beo Driste.
He wonede at Ernleie wid þan gode cniþte.
uppen Seuarne. merie þer him þohte.
faste bi Radistone þer heo bokes radde.
Hit com him on mode. & on his þonke.
þat he wolde. of Engelond þe ristnesse telle.
wat þe men hi-hote weren. and wan[e]ne hi comen.
Loweman gan wende. so wide so was þat londe.
and nom þe Englisse boc. þat makede Seint Bede.
Anoþer he nom of Latin. þat makede Seint Albin.
þat makede Austin. þat follo[s]t bro[s]te hider in.
Boc he nom þan þridde. an leide þar amidde.
Feþere he nom mid fingres. and wrot mid his honde. and þe soþe word sette togedere.
and þane hilke boc tock us to bisne.

Modern English

There was a priest was in the land. His name was Laghamon. He was Leoveath's son. May God be gracious to him.He lived at Earnley at a good church, upper Severn. He liked it there. Quite near to Radistone, he read services there
It came to him and as a serious thought that he would tell the story of England, their noble deeds, how they were called and where they came from. Laghamon did travel widely among the people, He took that English book that Saint Bede had made; Another he took, in Latin, that Saint Albin had made. And the fair Augustine, who brought baptism hither; A third book he took, and laid it alongside, He took feathers in his fingers, and he composed on parchment; And these three books he condensed into one.

The English in the section above is from the Otto manuscript, which is a little easier to read than the other surviving record, called the Caligula. This is later, and less reliable. It differs from the Otto quite markedly, as shown by the following two versions of the opening lines:

A prest was in londe. Laweman. was hote. he was Leucais sone. lef him beo Driste.
An preost wes on leoden; La3amon wes ihoten. he wes Leouenaðes sone; liðe him beo Drihten.

Laghamon. Stained glass window at the church of Areley Kings.

Brut is remarkable for the lack of words of French origin. There are only about 250 French words in the 30,000 lines the story. Scholars have not come to any agreement about these features. There are a few verb forms, such as “funde” as the past tense of “found” which may persist in modern Black Country.

Laghamon found most of his material from the French-speaking author Wace. He claims to be using other sources, but he seems to misunderstand Bede and the Latin of Albin. The author's history of the English people was quite fanciful. The Brut is Brutus, and other survivors of the Trojan war. They journey through southern Europe, before making their capital at New Troy or London. The line of kings includes Arthur, although Arthur is mainly a figure of Celtic legend.

Malvern in 1380

Piers Plowman is the title of an apocalyptic Middle English allegorical narrative, written by William Langland in the late 1300s. The author is thought to have started life in the Malvern Hills in Worcestershire, but to have later eked out a living in London.

The poem concerns the narrator's intense quest for the true Christian life, in the terms of the medieval Catholic mind. That quest entails a series of dream-visions and an examination into the lives of three allegorical characters, Do-Wel ("Do-Well"), Do-Bet ("Do-Better"), and Do-Best, who are sought by Piers, the humble plowman of the title. The ploughman describes stooping for a rest on a warm May morning on the Malvern Hills. There he falls into a reverie, and has a vision of a lady:

A lovely lady of leere in lynnen yclothed	
Cam doun from the castel and called me faire,	
And seide, “Sone, slepestow? Sestow this peple-	art thou asleep?
How bisie they ben aboute the maze?	see thou the people?
The mooste partie of this peple that passeth on this erthe,	
Have thei worship in this world, thei wilne no better;	
Of other hevene than here holde thei no tale”-	they do not want
I was afeed of hire face, theigh she faire were,	
And seide, “Mercy madame, what may this be to mene?”	
“The tour upon the toft” quod she, “Truthe is therinne,	
And wolde that ye wroughte as his word techeth.	
For he is fader of feith and formed yow alle	
Bothe with fel and with face and 3af yow five wittes	both with skin and face
For to worshipe hym therwith while that yow ben here.	gave you five senses
And therefore he highte the erthe to helpe yow echone	
Of woilene, of lynnen, of liflode at nede.....”	livelihood

Although not much later than Laghamon and Ancrene Wisse, Piers is considerably easier to understand for the modern reader. The right-hand column above gives only unfamiliar words. The vocabulary is mainly Anglo Saxon, with some Norse borrowings, e.g. “thei” instead of Saxon “heo”. The above passage may be read with a modern Dudley accent. “yow”, and “ben” are familiar. The “oo” sound (now found in words such as “bone” and “going”) seems to be used in several places where modern English has “oh”: “oother” and “mooste”. The distinctive West Midlands “o” vowel is seen in other passages in “bonke”, “sonne” and so forth.

French vocabulary comes in chunks, rather than in the middle of Germanic lines. The next two lines contain five French polysyllabic words, before returning to Germanic words.

“In mesurable manere to make yow at ese;	
And comaunded of his curteisie in commune three thynges;”	(words from French)
Are none nedfulle but tho, and nempne hem I thynke,	(named them)
And rekene hem by reson -- reherce thow hem after.	
"That oon is vesture from chele thee to save,	(clothing . . from chill)
And mete at meel for mysese of thiselve,	(meat at meal for myself)
And drynke whan thow driest	

“Comaunded of his curteisie in commune three thynges” has the repeated initial consonant required for alliteration, but the meter seems to be thrown out by the extra stressed syllables. There are also some Latin lines: The final line above, about alcoholic drink, is followed by a warning about Lot, drunkenness, and lechery.

What can we conclude from these texts about a West Midlands dialect of Middle English? The values of vowels are harder to compare than they would be in Old English. The difference between "o" in Mercian and "a" in West Saxon is known to have persisted in part until the present time. Laghamon in 1205 uses the "o" spellings for "hond", and "lond", though not for "man". However, Chaucer's London English in 1390 had the same spellings. It would be a major work of scholarship to compare Early Middle English in London and West Midlands, and this has not been done. Skeat in1912 (see Jordan, 1974) thought the greatest distinction of West Midlands dialect in Middle English was in the present and past participles of verbs. He claims that the present participle frequently ends in *–and,* and the past participle rarely has prefix *i-* or *y-*. However, these features are not very evident in Laghamon or Piers Plowman. Considerable scholarly effort would be needed to consider whether there is a West Midlands morphology.

The most obvious feature of writing in the Midlands in the 1300s is the strong use of Anglo Saxon. French is not well integrated. Laghamon and the writer of the Ancrene Wisse avoid French vocabulary, although they could probably read French. Langland places small sections of French and Latin in his English. Our best guess at this point is that writers in the 1300s who lived around the Severn wanted to insist on Anglo Saxon, and minimise the use of French.

Written Midlands English is hard to find after Chancery Standard English became the "high language" around 1425. Thereafter it continues mainly as a lower class spoken dialect.

5
Dudley around 1600

Migration of people

In Early Modern English times, who spoke the language that became Black Country? This is a difficult question, mainly because of the lack of written records. After Piers Plowman there is little writing from the area. We must therefore try to reconstruct local linguistic history from other records. Before coal working, there were probably only a few hundred people in the whole of the Black Country. Rowlands (1987) has a comprehensive account of the West Midlands from AD 1000 to the present, and estimates only 15,000 people in the whole of Staffordshire in 1327. Most of these would have been on fertile lowlands. Rivers and their banks were the main means of moving goods, so the population would have concentrated near to the River Severn, or in the far east of the county on the River Trent at Burton and Tamworth.

Population expansion is associated first with iron, and later with coal. Ironstone was mined in Walsall by migrant bloomers. The scale of ironworking was small and temporary, and the first permanent forge was at Kinver in 1373. Iron furnaces on a larger scale were established in the 1600s. An iron slitting mill in Hyde Mill, Kinver was slitting 400 tons a year in 1625. Industrial production at this time was mainly on a cottage industry basis. Nailers would make some income for half the year by laboriously slitting iron to make nails, and work on the land at spring and harvest time. Although coal extraction was already in evidence in Sedgley in 1273, and at various other places along the ten-yard seam, it was not necessary at that time except as a cheap domestic fuel. The inhabitants of Wednesbury were prohibited from spoiling the lord's corn by digging surface coal in the late fourteenth century. Coal came to replace timber for refining iron much later, perhaps in the 1600s. There were literally hundreds of coal pits in the area, mostly near-surface and small in scale. They are often unmarked, and occasionally make their existence known in modern times when a collapse occurs. The glass industry was brought to Amblecote by Lorrainers soon after 1600, attracted by clay and fuel.

Industry meant that the population had increased dramatically by the time of the English civil war. By 1662 the estimated total population for Staffordshire and Worcestershire was 40,000. This was 26% of the total for England and Wales, according to Rowlands' estimates from hearth tax figures. The really big expansion occurred during the industrial revolution. The population of the town of Dudley nearly doubled between the 1811 and 1831 censuses. This expansion was mainly led by steel. All steel and in the area has now ceased. Coal extraction ceased when Baggeridge colliery closed. The population then declined. The 2001 census shows 155,441 in Dudley, 146,407 in Sandwell, and 120,724 in Wolverhampton. Employment now includes many light industries but little heavy industry. Of the extractive industries, bricks continue to be made, road stone is quarried at Rowley Regis, and some glass is made.

So where did these immigrants and their language come from? While the glass workers came from another country, rather more moved a shorter distance, across the Severn. Ironworkers abandoned the backyard forges of the Forest of Dean to move to the new industrial centres. Villagers at Abdon Burf on the Clee Hills made a living for a time with surface coal, but the village was abandoned as the Staffordshire thick seam was developed. Ironbridge on the Severn is identified as the birthplace of the industrial revolution, where clay, iron, and coal could be found. It dwindled as canals further east provided more reliable water transport, and died after railways came. Presumably its iron and ceramics workers moved east. Birmingham, without major waterways, only started to develop with canals, and really expanded with rail after 1830. The probability is that migrants from Worcestershire, Staffordshire, Gloucester, Shropshire, Warwickshire and a few other places already spoke a similar dialect to that they would find in Dudley.

Dudley in 1570

But there is some West Midlands writing from the Early Modern English period. When a person died in Dudley, his or her executors made a handwritten record of their property. These inventories, and in some cases wills, were displayed in the county town – Worcester. These are preserved in the diocesan archives in Lichfield. The picture below is and extract from the will of Edward Blakemore, who died in Darlaston in 1639. This was the most legible of ten examined. A particular interest here is what appears to be the spelling of 'item' and 'and' with an 'o'; however, the same letter appears to be used in 'sheet'.

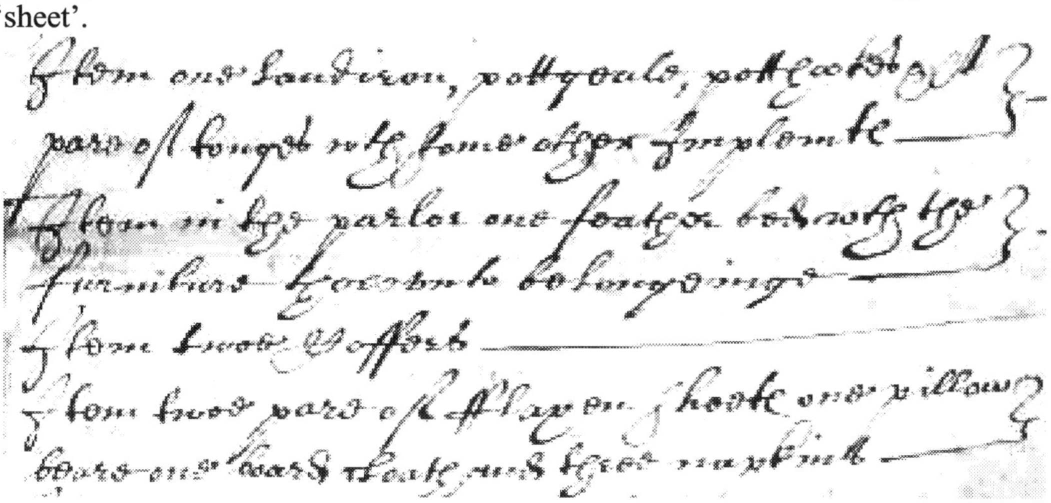

As you can see, handwriting from four centuries ago is difficult to read by a non-specialist. Fortunately for us, many were transcribed by a local historian John Roper (1968). His transcriptions can be found in the Dudley library archives at Coseley, and elsewhere. The next difficulty is working out how to pronounce what people wrote. There are few connected sentences in such an inventory, so we are not likely to find verbs and pronouns. Their main interest is vowels.

So how standardised or phonetic was writing? The spelling of the word "bedstead" argues that people wrote as they spoke, and did not know the standard spelling. Most inventories contains this word, which is written in numerous ways: "bedstid, bedstead, bedsteed, bedsteede, beddsteede". A single "e" is never found. We infer that most executors had not been to grammar school and learned Mulcaster's rules, so they tried to write as they spoke. They seem to have mostly pronounced it like the modern "steed", sometimes like "did", but never like "dead". "ee" is often pronounced short as "i" in modern BCD, and this seems to be the case in "bedstid". There are few other clear instances of this vowel. In Feredie's inventory below "Dudleye" is likely to be pronounced "ay" or "aye", unlike its modern standard pronunciation "ee".

"ay" and "air"

Unfortunately we cannot be confident about the characteristic BCD "air" and "ay" vowels, as the letter "e" is capable of several pronunciations. The relation between speech and spelling in Chaucer's writing around 1400 is fairly well understood, partly because of the rhymes. Yet is it was only recently realised that final vowels in Chaucer have to be pronounced: "shepe" would be pronounced "shay-puh", not as modern "sheep". Quite soon final "e" was used by printers to achieve the right length of typeface, and was not pronounced e.g. "ye olde shoppe". Mulcaster recommended in 1582 that a final "e" should indicate that the previous vowel is long, e.g. "hat" vs. "hate", and this is how we spell today. Grammar started to be taught in earnest in the late 1500s. King Edward VIth. grammar school in Stourbridge was founded in 1552.

"ŏ" and "a"

The range of possibilities for the letter "o" is slightly less ambiguous. "Ponne" for pan is common, but sometimes the standard English "a" is used e.g. "pan" and "hamer".

The diphthong "aye" is preferred to "oy" in the French loanword "joined". A "jined" or "gyned" bedstid is likely to be pronounced in the modern Dudley way.

"oo"

BCD now often uses "oo", e.g. "omboon" for "ham bone". This also seemed to be the case in Piers Plowman. The "loode of barke" in Feredie's inventory below suggests this "oo" sound. Dorothy Sutton's inventory in 1636 contains "tooles", but also "boockes" and "pootes".

Some words surprisingly have a short "o", where an "oo" is now found. John Cartwright the elder, d.1628 left a "spock shave". Alison Russon, widow, died in 1636 and left "spones" and "wodden bords". These and "bason" are more likely to have an "ŏ" than the modern "oo" sound.

"ow"

George Attwood d.1584, left "bowrdes" and "sawcers". The spelling of "tow" for number 2, and "fower" for number 4 suggest that the "ow" vowel was preferred over long "o". "two" and "twoe" are also found, but probably had quite different pronunciation.

Inventory of William Feredie, died 1559

The inventorie of such goodes and catle and implementes of householde as apperteinnde to William Feredie lately of Dudleye in the diocesse of Worcester April x . . . in 1559 valewed and preised by Thomas Lane Homfrey Smart and Thomas Fisher with others.

First in the haule - 2 bourdes with formes and trestile to ye same		*12s 0d.*
One peinted clothe:	*price*	*8d.*

In ye ketchen

4 brasse pottes:	*price:*	*8s. 0d.*
One ponne and tow skelletts and one little caldron		*6s. 0d.*
Two chaffyngdishes		*1s. 0d.*
16 peces of pewter 3 dishes and sawcers		*6s. 8d.*
One salt seller and 4 candlesticks and 2 pewter pottes		*2s. 0d.*
3 contrefette dishes one dosin trenen dishes and trenchers and one ladle		*8d.*
3 pales and 4 lomes		*2s. 0d.*
One spinning whele reele and a peire of cardes		*1s. 0d.*

In the chamber

One fetherbed and 1 flockebed with th'appurtenances		*15s. 0d.*
2 coverlettes:	*price:*	*8s. 0d.*
2 twillies:	*price:*	*3s. 0d.*
6 paire of sheets		*6s. 8d.*
4 bourde clothes:	*price:*	*6s. 0d.*
2 towelles:	*price:*	*2s. 0d.*
2 coffers:	*price:*	*2s. 0d.*

In ye tanhouse

One loode of barke		*1s. 4d.*
Lether there and toles to worke with		*£3 0s. 0d.*

In ye fielde

6 kine:	*price:*	*£6 8s. 0d.*
2 yearling:	*price:*	*13s. 0d.*
18 sheppe and 3 lambes:	*price:*	*£1 6s. 8d.*
One horse:	*price:*	*4s. 0d.*
2 swine:	*price:*	*5s. 0d*

Adebtes [sic]

Adam Wilson oweth	*£1 6s. 8d.*
William Kinges of Storbridge	*10s. 6d.*
ferne of Kinvare	*9s. 8d.*
Ric. Russell of hales owen	*15s. 0d.*

Totalis suma - £17 19s. 6d.

A few other documents exist from this time. The Manor of Enville has proceedings of courts in the 1400s and 1500s. Most of these manuscripts have yet to be transcribed or translated. Whilst most are in Latin, the steward of Ambulcott records this in his own English: “Thomas Hymlocke for lodyng more waynes with cooles that he ought – 4s”. The long “oo” characteristic of BCD is found in “coals”, though not in “lodying”, by contrast with Feredie’s inventory.

Writing from the late 1600s may be found in the pamphlet written by the Reverend Illingworth in 1678. It was expanded at some recent date by D.R. Guttery This is the account of a disreputable John Duncalfe, who denied stealing a bible and uttered an oath that God might rot his hands. Duncalfe soon developed a putrefying complaint of the limbs, which the author interpreted as God's wrath for the dishonest oath. However, Illingworth writes in the educated English of the time, so the interest of this story is its local characters and places rather than the dialect.

To conclude, a number of words can be pronounced in the modern Dudley fashion. The historical continuity of vowels is the subject of the next chapter.

6
Black Country Vowels

The Black Country way of saying the words "man" and "horse" is very different from standard English. Rather than thinking of them as different words, they are better thought as having different phonetics. There are about twenty vowels in Black Country, similar to the number in standard English. This will come as surprise if you learnt at school that English had 26 letters, five of which are vowels. A persistent problem of English spelling is that spoken language has many more vowels and combinations of vowels than we have letters. You can get an idea of the mismatch between speech and spelling by thinking of the sound called "schwa". This is the sound of both vowels in "button", and two of those in "computer". About half the vowels of spoken English are schwa, though you will probably never have heard of it unless you studied linguistics or speech therapy. It may correspond to a variety of letters.

Phonetics describes the way speech sounds are produced in the vocal tract, and also the acoustic properties of sounds. Vowels are produced when the vocal folds vibrate, and the position of the tongue makes a mouth cavity that resonates at a particular frequency. Consonants block the sound to some extent. Some consonants block the air flow completely before letting it go suddenly, and are described as plosives or stops. Others cause friction in the airflow and are called fricatives. A few others are like both consonants and vowels, as the tongue partially obstructs the air flow. These are called approximants.

Phonemes

Phonemes are sounds that convey meaning in the language. Phonemes cannot be defined by either acoustic or articulatory properties, as they occur in the brain. The words "bit" and "beet" to an English listener have two consonant phonemes in common, and differ by one vowel. A French listener would hear them as slightly different, but might think they are the same word, as French does not have a short "i". To an Arabic speaker "symbol" and "simple" are the same word. For an Urdu speaker "t" "d" and "dh" are three phonemes, where an English listener hears only two. Sometimes quite a broad range of sounds are heard with the same meaning, so the sounds are said to be allophones of the phoneme. In the case of the middle consonant in "butter", an English listener will accept Midlands, Cockney, or Irish allophones as the same phoneme, "t". However, an Urdu-speaking listener has an extra phoneme, and would hear the Irish pronunciation as a different word. In rapid speech many vowels are replaced by the unstressed schwa sound, so "was" becomes "wəz". This does not change the perception of the word, so schwa is an allophone for several vowels.

Some languages such as Hawaiian manage with less than a dozen phonemes. This created a problem when trying to say foreign words. Japanese used to be similar to Hawaiian, but increased its number of phonemes to 23 when it tried to incorporate Chinese words in the fifth century. English did not alter its phoneme inventory much when English speakers encountered French. The French nasals in "un bon vin blanc" and the "r" remain strange to us. The authoritative description of the sounds of English is by Peter Ladefoged. (2001). More on phonetics may be found in Clark and Yallop (1995).

Phonemes are acquired mainly in the first year of life. Human infants are extraordinarily good at detecting the contrasts in their parents' speech. Psychologists have called this ability a language acquisition device. Experiments that have shown phoneme discrimination by using the rate of a sucking a dummy as a sign of interest. An adult says a list of words such as “bit – bit - bit – pit - bit”. When the small change occurs when the voicing of “b” is removed, the infant often sucks faster. By the age of one year the infant can recognise virtually all the sounds of its maternal language, before it can speak hardly a word. After this age the child loses interest in new sounds, and concentrates on extracting the grammar. The phonetics of our own language seem “obvious”. After early childhood it is quite difficult to learn new phonemes.

Vowels

Vowels are described by the position of the tongue in relation to the roof of the mouth. The vowel quadrilateral shown below is defined by the four extreme positions of the tongue: “ee”, “a”, “ŏ”, “oo”.

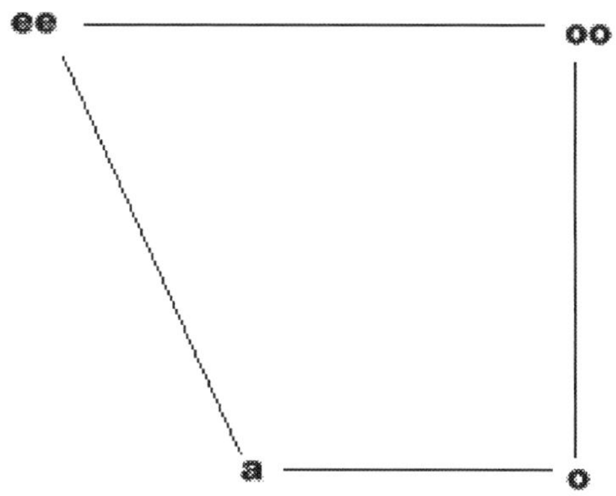

“ee” is produced when the tongue is as close to the ridge behind the teeth as it can be without making a consonant.
“a” has the tongue bunched at the front, but as open as it will go.
“ŏ” is produced when the tongue is back and open as far as it will go
“oo” has the tongue at the back and close; this is a deep sound.

Further shaping of the vowel is achieved by rounding the lips. The sound “aa” becomes long “o” by rounding the lips.

English RP (received pronunciation) has 20 vowel phonemes. It has six single vowels, and the rest are diphthongs. Ladefoged (2001) inserts 16 between the letters “b” and “d” to make 16 different words (although one is a part word, and one a name). Four in the final column finish with “r”, not a “d”. BBC English has to have these additional vowels, as it no longer has an “r” like American English.

bead	bard	booed	Boyd
bid	body	bud	beer
bayed	bawd	bird	bare
bed	budd(hist)	bide	byre
bad	bode	bowed	boor

The table below shows a provisional list of the main vowel phonemes of BCD. The first column gives a name for the vowel in ordinary Roman letters. The second column gives its symbol from the International Phonetic Alphabet. The third column gives example words.

There are several uncertainties in this list. One of these is the “u” sounds in “wust”, “wood”, “goose”, “school”. Southern English has two vowels here, which John Wells describes as FOOT and STRUT vowels. In Northern English foot and strut have the same vowel. Black Country sometimes has a diphthong in u sounds. This might be a phoneme, but might instead be an alteration needed for the meter, as discussed in chapter eight. Black Country sometimes uses tripthongs, as in “foyive”. However, this is probably not a phonemic difference, as it means the same as “faiv” and “five”.

Vowels of Black Country

BCD vowel	IPA symbol	Black Country examples
eeuh	iə	field, teeth, beer
ee	iː	three, green
i	ɪ	sid ('saw') wik ('week')
e	ɛ	make, take, sen ('say')
a	a	babby, saft
aye	aɪ	chice ('choice'), oyster, find, ail ('oil'), boy
air	æː	plairse ('place'), cairke, same, shape, shake, turn
air	ɛə	fairse, shairt, bacon, tayter
o	ɒ	oss, bonk, ommer, ond, bost, halibut, any, smash, stand
ar	ɑː	ar ('I', 'yes') arf, blart, mardy, taa, sound
u	ʊ	wust ('worst'), kup, bush, nuss ('nurse')
u	ʉ	wood, should, pun ('pound')
er	ɜː	erz ('hers'), return
ay	eɪ	grey, payz, kalied, steal, shape, teach, rilayse ('release')
or	ɔː	kor ('cannot'), gawk
uhoh	əʊ	wo ('will not'),
oo	uː	goose, bone, oon ('own'), stone
oy	ɔɪ	Friday, mither
ow	aʊ	yow, ow ('how')
ee-uh	ɪə	tew ('two')

Establishment of the vowel phonemes of BCD would be a substantial research task. It would require a decision on whether the following examples are diphthongs, or two syllables:

oo-uh	ʊə	school, fool

Displacement of Black Country Vowels

Ted Walker produced a large list of dialect 'words'. A large proportion of the distinctive 'words' of Black Country also occur in standard English, but with a different vowel. Many of these differences are quite systematic. Let us look at the biggest systematic differences next.

"o" for "a"

The best-documented feature of BCD words is the persistence of the "o" from Old English. Anglo Saxon words had *o* and *æ* (between *a* and *e*) as allophones. Eventually most dialects settled on the second sound, but the Midlands stayed with *o*. It is also found in Clee Hill dialect (Jenkins, 1982). The preference for *o* in the West Midlands is particularly clear when it s followed by a nasal sound *m* or *n*:

mon **'ond** **'ommer** **bonk** **ony** (any)

This pattern has changed little since the time King Offa fortified Mercia against the Welsh. It is a systematic part of the sound pattern of BCD, and would be applied to new, unfamiliar words. If the computing term Local Area Network came to be known as a "lan", it would naturally be pronounced in BCD as a "lon". The "o" is also found before other consonants, e.g.:

smosh **'ollibut** **'oss** **bost**

A few words are different in the opposite direction. BCD calls being silly "saftness". Several of these are words where "o" is followed by "p".

shap **drap** **saft**

"ay" for "ee" and "air" for "ay"

The "cup o tay" is one of the first phrases that strikes visitors. The same vowel difference occurs in quite a number of words. This pattern is easy to describe, but it needs some phonetics first! As previously mentioned, vowels can be described by whether the tongue is nearer the back or front, and how open or close the gap is. The following diagram shows the difference in pronunciation between standard English "ee" and BCD "ay" using the vowel quadrilateral. The left-hand column shows that standard English has the tongue very close to the roof of the mouth, and right at the front. The words are listed in the middle column. BCD has the tongue somewhat further away from the roof, but also at the front.

<table>
<tr><th>Standard English</th><th></th><th>BCD</th></tr>
<tr><td>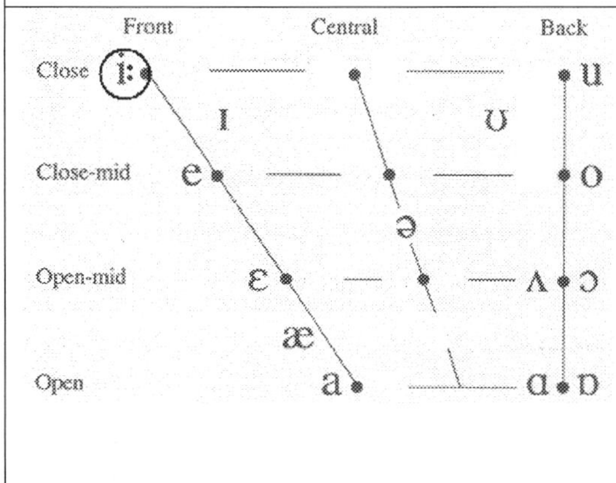
</td><td>ee v ay

peas,
tea,
weak,
teeth,
fleas,
steal,
teach</td><td>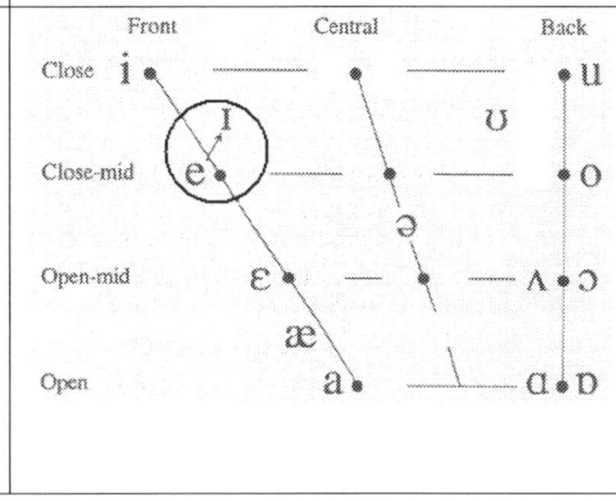
</td></tr>
</table>

The words in the next diagram show a second contrast, in words where Black Country has a fairly open single vowel (called a long ash) and standard English has a fairly close diphthong.

<table>
<tr><th>Standard English</th><th></th><th>BCD</th></tr>
<tr><td>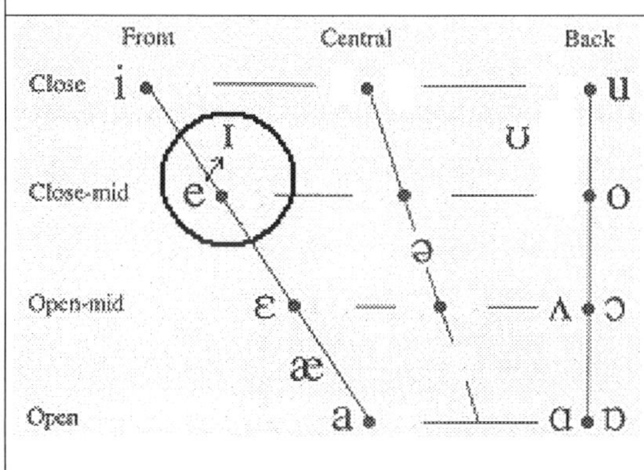
</td><td>ay v air

place,
cake,
state,
same,
bacon,
traipse</td><td>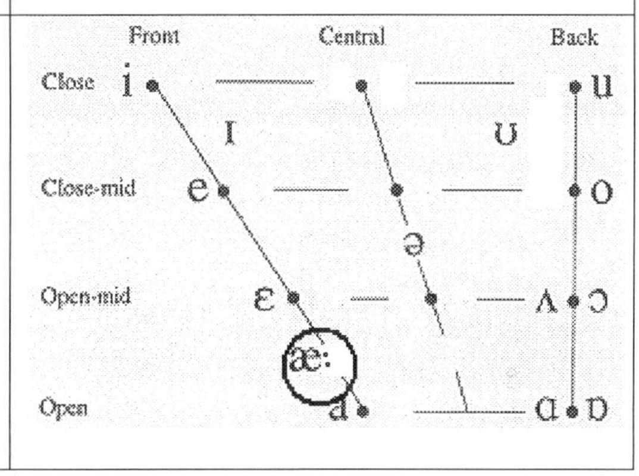
</td></tr>
</table>

These two sets are particularly interesting, as all the differences could be summarised by saying that the standard English vowel is "one step closer" than Black Country. This raises an intriguing possibility. What if Staffordshire and Worcestershire speakers resisted the Great Vowel Shift that occurred in standard English? This is a most interesting question, which will be considered again in a later chapter.

There are several other words that are pronounced distinctively, though there is less of a pattern. These include:

lung, strung	**long, strong**
babby	**baby**
boon, gooin'	**bone, going**

Borrowings from French

A sizable group of words that are pronounced differently in BCD and standard English generally come from French. BCD uses the *aye* sound compared with the standard *oy*. Some examples are shown below, with the French words from which they originate. The approximate Middle French pronunciation can be achieved by reading the letters afterwards with their standard English sounds.

jine	**joigner**	zhwan yay
bile	**bouillir**	boo weer
ail	**huile**	hoo weel luh
aister	**huître**	hoo wees tuh ruh
chice	**choisir**	shwa zeer

It can be seen that the French vowels are quite difficult for any English speaker, so it is not surprising they were adapted to the standard English *oy*. It is not clear how, when and where these borrowings occurred in standard English. While it is possible that Black Country borrowed them directly from Norman French, it is more likely that it borrowed them from standard English. Oysters were not common in Staffordshire in the past! The word boy, pronounced "bye" in BCD, is borrowed from another Germanic source rather than French, but has undergone the same sound change. There is a systematic contrast between BCD and standard English in the start point of the diphthong. BCD starts with a front vowel "a", and RP with the back vowel "o", but both finish with "i" . This seems to be the familiar o/a difference, but, puzzlingly, in the opposite direction. It should be possible to write one phonetic rule that tells us how to pronounce the o/a vowel according to the consonants before and after it. This has yet to be investigated, and is an exciting research possibility.

Consonants

Consonants are categorised by the role of the "articulators". The most important articulator is the tongue, and where it touches the roof of the mouth. The second articulator is the vocal folds, which can be vibrating or still. In each of the pairs below, the left-hand one is unvoiced, and the right-hand one is voiced. The third articulation is nasal, where air also comes out of the nose. This applies only to three sounds in the second row. The other articulator is the lips. The following table shows the consonants for Received Pronunciation (RP) in English. The symbols are those of the International Phonetic Alphabet. Most of them may be read as conventional Roman letters, except /j / which is pronounced "y". The letters θ and ð are the same as Greek, and pronounced as in "thin" and "this" respectively. "ʃ " is pronounced "sh". The two affricate symbols are as in "chin" and "gin". The upside-down "r" shows that most English dialects (but not Scots) have hardly any "r".

The table below shows the 24 consonant phonemes of RP.

	Bilabial	Labio-dental	Dental	Alveolar	Post - alveolar	Palatal	Velar	Glottal
Plosive	p b			t d			k g	
Nasal	m			n			ŋ	
Fricative		f v	θ ð	s z	ʃ ʒ			h
Affricate					tʃ dʒ			
Approx-imant				ɹ		j	w	
Lateral ap proximant				l				

A few unusual words arise in BCD where two consonants are run together in fast speech, a process called assimilation. One is the creation of a *dj* sound. In Old English dj was an allophone of /j/ occurring after /n/. The modern dj does not occur in many places. The only common examples are “Wedgebury” for Wednesbury, and this greeting:

“wharro bab, ah thort yow wuz jed” (“hello old friend, I thought you’d died”)

The consonants of Black Country are virtually the same as standard English. The main difference is the absence of an *h* sound and its replacement by nothing or *y*. “h-dropping” is a very strong marker for social class throughout England. Peter Trudgill (1974) showed this in different parishes of Norwich. Most of us know that lower-class people “drop their aitches”, so some people who are trying to improve their speech deliberately insert an aitch. Sometimes the effort produces an extra aitch, e.g. “hwhere”.

BCD goes much further than dropping an *h*, and inserts a *y* instead. The y (called a yod) occurs in places where it would be easier simply to leave it out, e.g. “use yer yed” and “full steam ayed”. The only phrase where a BC speaker will use an *h* is in “ship ahoy”. This trend is not well-described in English dialects. It might be called a yod-insertion. There is a paradox between the Mercian heavy use of “h”, and the complete absence of it in Black Country.

This chapter has looked at the smallest units of speech, its phonemes. It has been shown that characteristic vowels are the strongest feature of Black Country. The next chapter shows some further features – word endings.

7
Verbs: to be and not to be

Old English changed the endings of words (inflections) for grammar, and modern German still does so. Modern English uses position of words for most of its grammar, and has largely abandoned changing word endings. Verbs are the main parts of speech that still inflect. A modern English verb has five different endings, e.g. “sing, sings, singing, sang, sung”. Black Country has some very distinctive verbs, and may have four rather than five endings. The verb to be is very striking. At the beginning of the 21st. century the most common form uses “am” in most persons, and “is” in the third person singular, as follows:

	1S	2S	3SM	3SF	1Pl	2Pl	3Pl
Affirmative	ah’m	yow’m	ee’z	er’z	we’m	yow’m	they’m

In older speakers such as George there are several additional ways of saying “to be”. He still says “thou” when talking to one person. He then uses “bist” instead of “am”. But he also uses “bist” for other persons. There are more forms that come into play in negatives, and in tag questions. (Tags are questions that repeat the statement but negatively, inviting the listener to contradict it, e.g. “that’s good, isn’t it?”).

	1S	2S	3SM	3SF	1Pl	2Pl	3Pl
Negative	ah bay	yow bay	ee ain’t	er ay	we ay	yow ay	they ay
		thee bisn’t			we bay		
	bin I	bin yow	duz ee	duz er	bist we	bin yow	bist they
Tag	bist I	am yow		iz er	am we	bist yow	bin them
		dun yow			bay we	am yow	
		bist yow			ay we	ay ya	

There are more non-standard features here. There are negative contractions such as “bay”, which means “am not”, but in a single word. We shall come back to this, but let us look first at where “bin” and “bist” came from.

The two distinct forms, “wesan” and “beon” were described in chapter three. Standard English stayed mainly with wesan, but lost “sind” in the plural. This is still the standard German form. At some point the Scandinavian plural “are” replaced it. Many dialects kept “beon” and do not use “wesan”; Somerset is one we notice particularly. Black Country uses both verbs: from wesan “am” is used for every person except “er is”; from beon “bin” is used for most persons; confusingly, “bist” can also be used for most persons.

The Survey of English Dialects

So are Black Country verbs an island, or are these uses found in neighbouring counties? A major survey of English dialects was undertaken by Professor Orton of Leeds University, together with Professor Dieth of Zurich. They interviewed older male farm workers at many points all over England. Their results were maps showing the areas which shared the same forms (called isoglosses). The maps use traditional county boundaries, and not modern urban areas such as the County of West Midlands. So you have to look for the old country boundaries of Staffordshire, Worcestershire, and Warwickshire in the following pictures. The first person forms "I am" and "ah bin" both occur in neighbouring counties. The second person forms are shown in the next map.

Isogloss map of second person singular, redrawn from Orton and Dieth (1962).
The most recognisable features are the Severn estuary and the Wirral peninsula.

'you are' was spoken in
Staffs and Leics
'thee bist' was used in
Worcs and Gloucs.
Black Country uses both these, but not 'thou art' and 'you bin'.

When we come to the third person form, there is only "he is" and no "he be". "Is" was usual in most parts of the Midlands. The nearest alternatives "he be" and "he bin" are found only in west Shropshire.

The real complexity comes when we look at the way "they are not" is said in neighbouring counties. Orton's map below shows twelve different ways of saying it, four of which are near the Black Country.

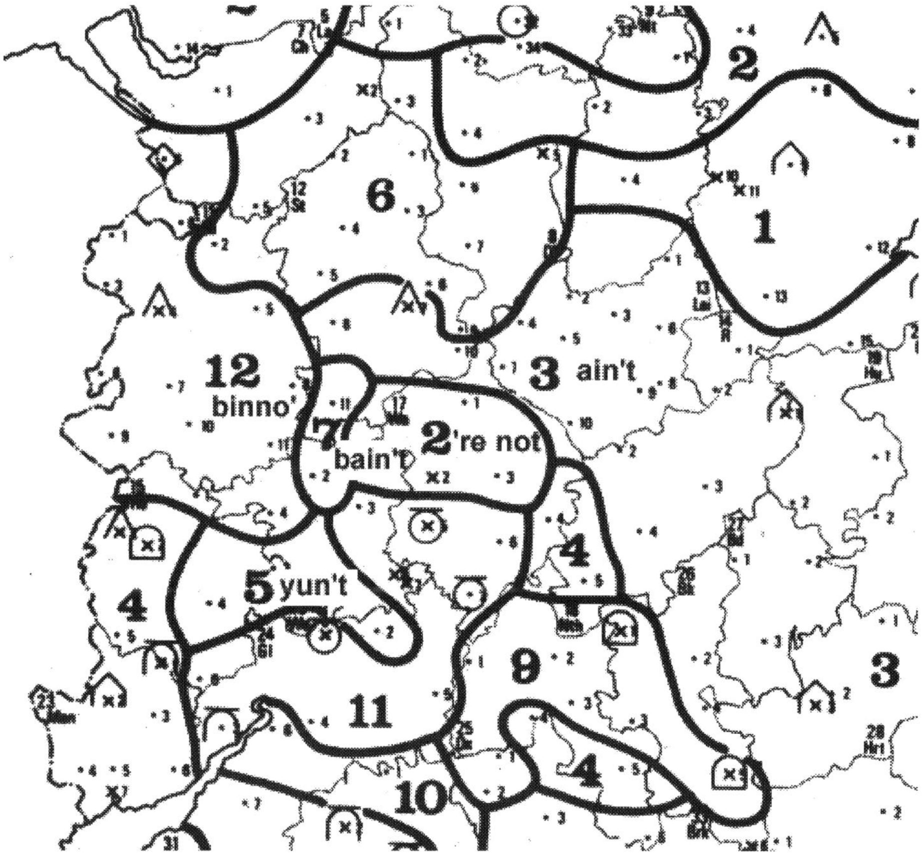

Isogloss map of third person plural negative

Other irregular verbs of BCD

Some other common verbs have different conjugation in the West Midlands, e.g. "it cotch'd 'im", "'er was took", "ah fun it", "we sid it". Some of these may be continuations from Midlands Middle English.

	Present	Simple past	Past participle
find	find	found, fun	found
come	come	come	come
break	brairk	broke	broke
make	mairk	med	med
catch	cotch	cotch'd	cotch'd
give	give	gi'd	gi'd
ride	ride	rid	rid
pick	pick	pick'd, puck	pick'd

Differences in the simple past mostly involve using the "-ed" ending where standard English changes the vowel, e.g. "gi'd" for "gave". This is described as remaining weak, which means following the general rule. Many English verbs became weak in Middle English, when it was a low language under Norman French. Unusually, there are a couple where Black Country changes the stem and Standard English is weak. "Fun" as the past tense of "found" is fairly common in Dudley, and "puck" instead of "picked" is heard occasionally. "Funde" as the past tense of "found" is the form used in Laghamon. The verb "catch" includes the "gh" sound that has disappeared from English but not Scots. Standard English dropped the sound, but kept the "gh" letters. BCD also dropped the sound, but seems to have replaced the missing "gh" with "tch".

The missing past participle in BCD

Standard English uses a past participle in phrases like "I have taken" or "she was chosen". Grammar specialists used to think that English had underlying tenses like those of Latin, so English was taught as having a perfect tense. Perfection is now described as an aspect rather than a tense, so the form "I have eaten" is now called the present perfect, and "I had eaten" is the past perfect. It is doubtful whether Black Country has a past participle. In all the examples above informants used the same verb ending after "have" as when saying the simple past.

Old English did not have a perfect. English developed a perfect by conjugating the verb "to have" with the stem of the main verb, in this fashion: "I have/ you have/ he has + eaten". This use of "have" as an auxiliary developed in late Old English in examples like the following:

> Ic hœbbe þone fisc gefangene ("I have the fish as caught")

"Am" was also used, but "have" gradually replaced it in Middle English. Verbs of motion like "go" took the auxiliary "am" e.g. "I am gone" is found in Shakespeare. "I have gone" became standard after several centuries. French also uses the verb "avoir" in this way, but more extensively than English. French made a future tense by using the future endings of avoir – "j'aurai, tu auras", etc. – as suffixes on the main verb, to make "je mangerai, tu mangeras", etc. German also developed a perfect: "Ich sah" and "Ich habe gesehen" are two ways of saying "I saw", though they have merged again and now mean virtually the same thing.

Black Country seems to have resisted the perfect in standard English. It is probably not a question of laziness. Dialect speakers go to some trouble in phrases like this:

> "if er'd a-knew it was yer birthday, er'd a-bought yer a present"

The speaker knows that in school he would have been corrected, and told to say "if she had known . . .". Yet he persists in following a different rule. But what is it? "A-knew" might be using "of" as though it were a verb. Many English people do this, saying things like, "if I'd of known". This might be a misunderstanding that arises because "have" and "of" sound the same when they are not stressed. There is another possibility, that it is a persistence of the "y-" prefix from Middle English. Chaucer describes a man with a smooth chin as "late y-shave". Black Country also uses an "a-" prefix with the present participle, e.g. "ee was a-cummin round the bend . . . ".

The a-prefix was also described by Margaret Rock in 1974 in these examples:

> "if there'd a-been children" and "we'n just bin a-laughin".

It seems likely that Black Country did not follow standard English in extending the possessive verb "have" as an auxiliary verb to make a new tense. It finds ways of using the simple past tense to show completed actions.

Negative contractions

The negative contractions e.g. *dun* and *doh* are a well-known aspect of BCD. They are usually found rather unattractive by outsiders. The main ones are:

Standard English	BCD affirmative	BCD negative
be	bin	bay, ay
was	was	wor
do	do	doh
did past	did	day
can	can	cor
will	'll	woh

"Mo" for 'must not' and "shor" for 'should not' may also be heard, but are not common.

Negative contractions in a single syllable are highly unusual, and possibly unique to this dialect. Standard English used to have negative contractions, which are described in detail by Hogg (2004). "Nis" meant "is not" and "nolte" meant "does not want". There is a still a trace of this in the phrase "willy-nilly" (wolte–nolte). Negative contractions died out by about 1500. The origin of Black Country contractions is unknown. They might follow the introduction of "ain't" into standard English around 1780, and extend it further to "bain't" and "dain't". The way the contractions are made is by changing to a long vowel rather than putting an "n" at the front, so they are not a direct continuation of negative contractions from Early Middle English. But they may have developed to fill the gap left when the other contractions disappeared.

There is very little difference between the affirmative and negative forms. The only difference is the length of the vowel. The answer to "Can you keep the furnace shut while I get past?" might be "ah con" or "ah cor". A misunderstanding might be disastrous. Both Jespersen (1946) and Cheshire (1998) show that languages tend to add emphasis to negatives to avoid misunderstanding. English speakers used to add say "na", but found they had to add "whit" to be understood. This "na – whit" became standard, contracted to "not". This requirement to give emphasis continued. Then people had to find another emphatic to add onto "not". French speakers added "pas" to "ne", so "ne-pas" became standard. The lack of emphasis in BCD is puzzling.

Pronouns

The other class of words that inflect is pronouns. English nouns no longer have object and indirect object cases, but keep only "-s" for possession. Pronouns keep three cases – subject, object, and possessor.

The unusual pronouns of BCD are "er" and "we". "Er" is used both as subject and object, where standard English uses "she" for subject, and "her" for object. "We" is used as subject, occasionally as object, and also for possession, as in "we held we babby in we arms". This is a simplification, like the Yorkshire use of "have us teas", or the Jamaican use of "me" for "I". This habit of lower class dialects to simplify may be one reason English lost many of its case endings under Norman French rule.

person → case ↓	1S	2S	3SM	3SF	1Pl	2Pl	3Pl
subject	ah, oy	thee, yow	ee	er	we	yow	they, them
object	me	thee, yow	im	er	us, we	yow	them, em
ownership	my'n	yowern	iz'n	er'n	our'n	yowern	theyern

The pronouns that show ownership are interesting because of their "en" endings. In Old English a noun showed ownership or that it was plural by adding "en". In Modern English "s" is used for both. To compare two children's drawings, a standard English speaker could say, "hers is better than his". This would also be clear to the Black Country speaker, but he feels obliged to add an "en", saying "er'n is better than iz'n". This suggests that the Anglo Saxon intuition that "en" shows ownership still persists. The Mercian nouns on page 13 mostly had vowel endings in the nominative case, but added an –n in the genitive singular. The "en" for plurals also persists more than in Standard English. It has only "oxen" and "brethren", while the plural of "flea" is sometimes "fleen" in Black Country. –En adjectives are also heard, such as a "boughten cake".

Sentences such as "I'll get me one o' them" need a mention here. This use of the pronoun (called an external reflexive) is not now found in standard English, but continues to be a feature of many Germanic languages.

In this chapter we have looked at word endings, or what linguists call morphology. We have seen that Black Country English has followed many changes in standard English, but resisted some and kept some features of Early Middle English.

8
The rhythm of speech

Stress and meter

Meter is the distribution of stress across a whole utterance or sentence. The subjective impression of stress combines pitch, loudness, and length. It is rather difficult to define stress, and it cannot yet be measured by electronic means. We are aware when a stress convention has been broken. For example, national newsreaders sometimes say "Wolverhampton" with the same stress as "Wolverton", and it immediately sounds odd. It takes much longer to work out what the stress pattern is. Black Country has a distinctive rhythm to it, giving the impression of short words and a lack of musicality. The meter of BCD has hardly been studied, so the readers who spoke the dialect as children may try the examples in the following pages, and test whether they fit their intuitions. The native speaker's intuitions about meter form part of the competence, but they have never been made explicit. They are likely to have persisted for generations.

A common belief about urban dialects is that they stem from a "noisy environment". As a hypothesis this is rather unclear: do people fighting noise speak with lower or higher pitch, longer or shorter vowels, sharper or more slurred consonants? It is also what Saussure calls a "diachronic" question: it needs historical evidence, which we are unlikely to find. There is no straightforward way of testing this belief.

Although we cannot define stress very clearly, most people can agree most of the time which of two syllables has stronger stress, and which weaker. We can get some idea about the stress patterns of natural speech by looking at poetry patterns. Poets deliberately choose stress patterns for effect. A stressed syllable can be marked in various ways: by writing "S" below the syllable, by bold typeface, or by putting a grave accent above it. The examples below use a backslash "\" over a stressed syllable, and an "x" for a less-stressed syllable. This is relatively crude. The complexity of English stress would be better represented with "1" for the weakest, going up to "6" for the strongest stress.

A common poetic pattern is a sequence of pairs of weak and strong syllables. A consistent strong-weak (trochaic) pattern is one of the simplest. Longfellow's Song of Hiawatha has a very memorable meter because of this trochaic pattern:

```
\ x   \   x \ x \ x
By the shore of Gitche Gumee,

\ x  \ x  \  x  \ x
By the shining Big-Sea-Water
```

Romantic poems such as Shakespeare's sonnets often use a weak-strong (iambic) pattern. The following uses five such pairs (and is therefore called an iambic pentameter).

```
x  \  x  \   x   \ x \ x   \
Shall I compare thee to a summer's day?
```

We have said several times that English has a basically Germanic pattern, which has had to incorporate French. This is true of vocabulary, but it also probably true for meter. The vocabulary of BCD is Germanic, so the underlying meter of Black Country may be assumed to be Germanic. Stress in Germanic languages falls on the root syllable. This is the first syllable, except when preceded by an unstressed vowel as in past participles. Modern German words usually stress the first syllable, except where the prefix is separable, e.g. ab-, auf- . However, Black Country is mainly monosyllabic, so any rule about meter would apply to sentences rather than words.

Some differences have developed between English and its cousins such as Friesian, Swedish, or Yiddish. English has departed from other Germanic languages in becoming highly isolating, meaning that it uses prepositions and other connecting words where those languages would make a compound with inflection. Syllables starting with a vowel in English can be elided (slurred) with the previous word. This is now different from German, where a definite break has to be inserted if the word starts with a vowel. For example, all the sounds in "on the Earth" may join, whereas "an die Erde" has to have a definite break, called a glottal stop, before "Erde".

Alliterative verse was very important in Old English. The significance of this, according to Baker (2003) is that alliteration followed the normal meter of speech. Acceptable verse patterns followed normal speech rhythms. The final rhymes of modern poetry come from Romance languages, and do not sound good with unstressed Germanic endings. Recall that Piers Plowman, Laghamon and others tried to use the alliterative way of writing. It essentially involves matching the left edges of stressed syllables. An alliterative verse has a half line that has two strongly stressed syllables or "lifts". The first lift in the second half-line must alliterate with either or both of the lifts in the first half-line. The second lift does not alliterate.

French has a quite different metrical pattern. It is often described as a syllable-timed language, in which syllables are all about the same length, and more equally stressed. The French pattern may be heard in long words that have been borrowed from French into English, such as "communauté Européenne", which becomes "European community":

French:	yew – rrho – pay – en – nuh	ko – myew – no - tay
English	yewr – up – ee- un	kom – yewn – ut -ee

French syllables are likely to start with a consonant. (This extends to a hint of an extra final syllable, as in "nuh" above, which avoids finishing on a consonant). English syllables prefer to start with a vowel, as in "European" above. Suffixes that are from Germanic, e.g. "–ness", are unstressed, while those from French, e.g. "–able", attract stress. You can hear the difference in "likeness" and "likable".

The awkwardness of fitting French syllable-timed polysllables into a Germanic stress-timed meter gave major problems for standard English. The general solution was to reduce the stress on later syllables of French loan words. Black Country has made far fewer accommodations to French, so the Anglo Saxon pattern should be more audible.

Idioms are not a good way to discover meter, as they include emphatic stress, in additional to normal metrical stress. The following is a description by George of his childhood:

\ x \ x x \
Ar, when I wuz a lad.

\ x \ x \ x \ x x \ x
Ah wuz born in Darlaston, of a babby.

\ \ x \ x \ x
Ah 'ad a brutal fairther.

\ x \ x x x \ x
Ee wuz no good to me mother.

x \ x \ x x \
Ee used ter knock 'er abaht.

\ x \ x x \ x x \
Ah remember when ah was a lad

\ x \ x x \ \ x \ \ x
Ah wuz only abaht three 'n a half, fower

x \ x x \ x \
But ah con remember back . . .

The main impression is that stress usually falls on the first syllable of a noun or verb. The stressed syllable is rarely any other part of speech. This conforms to the Germanic pattern. The stressed syllable is usually followed two or three unstressed syllables. There are exceptions: "always" has initial stress. Quite often the final syllable is stressed, e.g. "lad", and "back". Occasionally two stressed syllables may occur in sequence. Sometimes Black Country approximates to alliterate verse:

Marry the **mis**kin for the **muck** (and get)

Pizened wi the **pi**zen in it

Splitting syllables

There may be another metrical pattern in the Black Country sentence: a requirement for final syllables. One very distinctive feature of the Black Country dialect is the tendency to split syllables into two. School may be pronounced "skewul", and town as "towun". However, this may not happen everywhere in the sentence. "Schoolwork is boring" is not split, while "I get bored in school" is split.

This possibility can be tested by asking a Black Country speaker to repeat a sentence using words of French origin. The following example has several words with Strong–Weak–Weak stress (called dactyls). The words are "Pam-uh-luh", "byoo tee-ful", "pritt-i-lee", and "sek-rit-ree". These three dactyls require the speaker to finish with an unstressed syllable. If this phrase is repeated several times in a Chinese whisper, it is predicted that the three phrases will change to give a final stressed syllable with rising pitch. Readers who speak the dialect are invited to try this experiment.

"The MD's secretary is called Pamela. She's really beautiful. Her always dresses prettily".

Further clues about metrical rules may sometimes be inferred from children's mistakes. The following phrase was reported in a boy from Pensnett by a primary school teacher:

> "Please Miss, can ah wash me anudz?"

The humorous effect of this sentence hides its real interest. This child seems to know a metrical rule, but has over-generalised it. Perhaps he knows that the dialect requires a stressed final syllable, which starts with a vowel. Native speakers share such intuitions, which linguists call a phonological rule. The rule has never been written down in a grammar, and nobody has taught it. In this case it might be: "stress the final syllable, raise its pitch; finish with a consonant if you can". The child has achieved this, and finished with a weak-strong syllable pair, at the price of altering the word in a novel way which other speakers do not accept.

BCD seems to be a very conservative dialect. Conservatism probably acts through trying to fit foreign influences into the dialect meter. The basic strategy of English in incorporating French loanwords is to give them Germanic stress. "Secretary" becomes S - W - W in English. "Société" also has four equally stressed syllables, but becomes "society" with stress on the second in English. If Germanic stress had been strictly applied, it might have been "soss-ee-ut-ee". Such four-syllable words are still fairly uncomfortable for Black Country meter, so a word such as "club" will be used if possible. Another strategy for French loanwords is to clip the ending. "Pup" started off as French "poupée", which means doll. English speakers (wrongly) thought it was a childlike form like "dolly" or "Jimmy", and removed the "ee". Further study of these effects can be found in the Cambridge History of the English language edited by Hogg (1992), and the work of Otto Jespersen (1946). This Danish professor has a masterful grasp of earlier forms of English.

BCD preserves very old patterns of meter and phonetics and resists modern influences.

Conservatism is not a conscious process, unlike the campaign for Welsh language.

In conclusion, we may say that Black Country has an underlying meter that causes it to favour words of Germanic origin. It is likely that the attempt to maintain its preferred meter is the main reason it resisted the change required by French. Although there are a small number of words not found in standard English, many of these will disappear as agricultural livelihoods pass into history. The meter and vowels will persist longer. The metrical pattern has not been researched, and we cannot define the stress rules with confidence at present. Research on it should be exciting.

9
From Mercian to Black Country

The previous chapters have described how Black Country has rules governing vowels, verbs, pronouns, and meter. These rules have been partly brought out by interrogating the competence of dialect speakers. This is what the famous linguist Ferdinand de Saussure calls a "synchronic" question (at the current time). Speakers have little idea where their mother tongue came from, and are surprised to find it has grammatical rules. As a reader you may have been startled to read that standard English has 44 phonemes, and no future tense. You are nonetheless able to use these phonemes, and apply an aspect rule to refer to future events. This language competence goes very deep in the human brain, and we can test it.

The other question is "diachronic": when and where did these features originate? Are they simplifications of standard English that emerged a generation or two ago, or are they persisting effects of much older patterns? Simplification often happens in lower-class speech, so the verb ending "they am" might be a recent generalization, in which first person is generalised to the third person. But they might also be a continuation of "wesan", resisting the import of Norse "are" into English. How can we tell?

The diachronic question can be partly answered by population history and scraps of writing. The speech community is more likely to have been Severn Valley than Black Country. Before 1350 there were probably only a few dozen people living on the high ground around Dudley. More people lived in the villages along the Severn. Migration away from the river might have started in the 1400s. Migrants brought sheep and pigs, and worked the land for some of the year, so they used Staffordshire and Worcestershire agricultural words. Their cottage industries included making charcoal and slitting iron into nails. Coal became valuable somewhat later, probably for glass blowing after 1600, then for smelting. Colliers moved round the area of the Staffordshire thick seam as pits were worked out. Dialect speakers were labourers. They did not write down their speech, as there were infrequent reasons to do so. Their children shared the language throughout the coal-working area. By the time of the heyday of steel the dialect was the common language of some hundreds of thousands of people. A hundred years ago a cable-maker from Cradley might not have made himself understood 20 miles from his home, but the dialect is nowadays quite diluted.

Vowels show considerable continuity. Piers Plowman and Dudley inventories do suggest that BCD's distinctive vowels have been in use for several hundred years. The vowels of Black Country are similar to those of standard English, but they are often displaced, usually with the tongue one step more open.

The BCD negative contraction probably dates from Modern English times. The forms "bay" and "day" are very likely to have come from "bain't" and "dain't", the partly contracted forms found in Brummie. "Ain't" and other contractions came into standard English around 1780. It is unlikely that they continue the Mercian negative contraction "nis". However, this does not entirely solve the puzzle. The BCD contractions "ah con" and "ah cor" are too close. Jespersen's argument is that emphasis requires another word, e.g. "ah con never!". This does not happen. Although the BCD contractions are unlikely to be modifications of Mercian "nis" "nolte" and "noebbe", they might fill a gap left by the disappearance of negative contractions in standard English.

The inflections of verbs and pronouns are more difficult to date. The use of "her" for both "she" and "her", and "we" for "our" might be a simplification. Other English dialects often manage without three forms of personal pronoun, e.g. Yorkshire "us'll have us teas". However, the OE female pronoun was "hea", which changed via "hya" and "shya" into "she" in standard English. BCD may simply be more conservative, and stayed closer to "hea". In the verb "to be", BCD went part of the way with London English in dropping "heo" in favour of Norse "they", but dropped "sind" in favour of "am" and did not take up "are".

There are research questions for linguists here. Some of these questions can be answered by interrogating the competence of native speakers, and others by greater attention to historical documents. Hypotheses about the main features of the dialect are set out in a rather formal way below.

Defining features of the dialect

	Feature	Example
Phonetic	o/æ → o before nasal	mon, 'ommer, bonk
	o/æ ? before stops	oss, rot; shap, drap
	ay for ee	tay, pays
	air for ay	fairse, baircon
	yod, aitch deletion	yed, 'oss, 'er
	Germanic meter	mind 'ow yow cross the 'oss road
	final stressed VC	skewul, towun
Morphological	no past participle	if er'd a-knew, it was took
	-ve contractions	bay, wor, day
	both wesan & beom	bist in most persons exc. 3S
	ME pronouns	er (3S), yow (2S and 2PL)
	-n for possession, plural	fleen, izern, boughten
Lexical	Anglo-Saxon ~ 85%	ail, pizen, pup etc. < 15%
	distinctive BCD words	bostin; get shut on
	ME persistence	fittle, clammed, loose, mardy
	husbandry words	blart, bobowler, shed, tiddler, poke
	deprecations	yampy, gawby, nincompoop
	alcohol words	olla leg, arf cut, kaylied, well-oiled
	idioms	round the Wrekin, op and a catch

There is much interest in documenting minor languages at the present time. One estimate is that there are 6,500 languages in the world, of which half will suffer language death in the next two generations. The existence of world-wide communication favours the spread of a few major languages. We are of course aware of the spread of English, but Mandarin, Spanish, Russian, and Swahili continue to replace other languages. National language is displacing dialects. This was happening in England after 1425. In Italy this has only happened since national television became widely available.

But is Black Country a dialect in terminal decline? One consideration is employment. Workers who lived around the big steel mills could spent most of their lives using only the dialect. The break-up of such closed industrial villages means that nearly every adult has to be able to speak and write fairly standard English to have any kind of job. Dialect is used only at home and with one's peers. A second consideration is the disappearance of words from agriculture. Most of these old Staffs and Worcs agricultural words are no longer recognised by young people, but a handful of distinctive words are surviving with metaphorical senses.

While vocabulary of Black Country is shrinking, its phonetics, phonology and morphology remain strong. Small children in Tipton, Lower Gornal or Pensnett continue to acquire the grammar rules described in the table above. This is often despite the best efforts of teachers to teach "good English"! Primary education does not recognise Black Country as a legitimate grammatical dialect. This may put dialect speakers at a disadvantage, as they in effect have to learn a second language in order to learn to read.

There are implications for self-esteem, research, and educational policy. Black Country speakers could take pride in their Anglo Saxon roots. A number of possible grammar rules have been suggested rather tentatively in this book. Dialect research is greatly needed. At the educational level, it would help children's learning if the speech of the neighbourhood were valued, and the separate grammar were acknowledged. We will be interested to see how readers react to these ideas.

Appendix: dialect words

This list is derived mainly from Ted Walker's undated dictionary. Other sources were the book *Proper Brummie* by Chinn and Thorne (2002), and a BBC local radio web-site. Their origins were researched in the Oxford English Dictionary Online, as it was in 2005, and the six volume dialect dictionary of Wright (1898-1905). The abbreviations for counties (e.g. Rnf = Renfrew) are where Wright found publications using them. Authors that do not appear elsewhere are from the OED online.

'Argey-Bargey': argument, quarrel; from argle-bargle in 19th. century Scots; Wright records in Rnf. Ayr.Lnk.; now widespread.

'Baum' (Walker): daub, smear; this may be balm, originally to embalm, and to soothe or alleviate pain in Shakespeare.

'Bawk': confuse (Chinn); this may be a variant of baulk, to hinder or place a balk in the path of someone.

'Bawby': a simpleton (Chinn); may be a variant of booby, meaning a lubber, a stupid fellow, though the vowel change is not regular.

'Berk', 'Baerk': a fool; abbreviation of Berkeley (or Berkshire) Hunt, rhyming slang; earliest OED entry is 1936.

'Bibble': a pebble, stone, or fossil in Stf. only; not recorded in OED.

'Bladder': something round and hollow; includes football, bagpipe, purse; Sc. Irel. NHb. Yks. (not Stf.); 'Bladdered': drunk.

'Blather': blather and blether mean to talk foolishly or indiscreetly, especially in Scotland; Old Norse blaðra means to talk indistinctly; other senses are S.Yks. to besmear with blood, An, Nrf. to blot in writing, N.Yks. to make foul; a noun meaning any liquid or semi-liquid, usu. disgusting; the BBC web-site records this as meaning drunk, presumably a phonetic variant or mishearing of bladdered.

'Blart': of sheep and cattle, to bellow; of children, to cry, lament, roar. Chs, Stf, also Der. War. Wor.

'Bloke': man, fellow; OED gives entries from 1862, etymology unknown; not found in Wright.

'Boff': an alarm, sudden shock; recorded in Yks. by Wright.

'Bost': past of verb, also bosted, bosten; Wright says a mild imprecation in Stf. War, Chs. etc.; used in 19th. century as a stage in wood carving; also broken.

'Bostin': excellent; the OED by contrast gives it a pejorative sense, a variant of boast, with primary sense to lift up one's voice; speak ontentatiously; threaten, bully, the ME sense was ostentatious or vainglorious speaking, e.g. Wyclif c.1380 "the gospel telliþ of bosting of a proude man".

'Bob-owler': any large moth; Stf. War. Wor.; hence metaphorically a person who stays out late in the evening.

'Bobby-dazzler': anything striking or excellent; a fine handsome woman; also a silly person, a mad action. Yks. Lan. Chs. Stf.

'Cake': oatcake, bread etc.; simpleton; 'Cakey': adj. silly; 'Cake hole' slang for mouth.

'Cag-handed': clumsy, left-handed; see keck-handed.

'Cag-mag': a meddlesome woman (War. Wor. Glo.); other senses include tough meat Yks.; loiter, Nts.

'Cherf': scold (BBC); probably a phonetic variant of chaff, meaning to banter in a non-angry way; first recorded in 1890s.

'Chobble': to chew, bite into small pieces. Glo. War. Wor. Yor.

'Chow-row': grumble or scold; possibly 'chowre', OED entry for 1567; not found in Wright; see Jower.

'Chuffed': pleased; Wright records this in Wm. Stf. Yks.; the OED records it in the 1960s; chuff is Adj. and Adv. meaning proud, conceited, pleased, a verb to plump out the cheeks, and a noun meaning the anus or a stupid person.

'Clammed': to be very hungry, ailing; phonetic variant of Old High German clem, to pinch; for example, Ben Jonson (1599) " Hard is the choise when the valiant must eate their armes, or clem"; the simple verb hardly appears before 1600, but is widely spread in the forms *clem* and *clam* over the northern half of England from Westmorland to Leicester, and from Lincoln to Hereford; its distribution makes it possible that it is of Norse origin.

'Clarnit': to play the fool; not found in Wright or OED; it may be a phonetic variant of clown it; a transitive form of clown is found after 1891.

'Clobber': clothes; in OED from 1860s; OE forces slang from 1944; Clob means clod of earth in Wor. Glo , but sense of clothes was not in Wright's time; also means to hit.

'Clock': as verb, to strike someone; Australian slang, 1941; as noun, the face; the words 'clock' and 'dial' are both used to mean the human face from the late 19th. century.

'Collywobbles': diarrhoea, colic; a semi-comic term for minor ailments; in general use.

'Conk': the nose, in War., Wor.; recorded in 19th. century with this meaning; possibly form French conch, shell; the head in Yks.

'Crerta': whisky (BBC web-site); not found in Wright or OED, needs attestation..

'Cuffy' (BBC web-site): scruff; not found in Wright or OED; cuff is the nape of the neck in Yks. Irel. Sc.; see below for confusion between scruff, scurf.

‘Donkey’s ’ears’: a long indefinite period of time; Sc. War. Oxf. Dev. Guer.

‘Donny’, ‘Danny’: hand, when talking to children; in Stf. War Hrf. Yks. (Wright); not in OED.

‘Es’: during these times; in W.Som, according to Wright; not in OED.

‘Fanaigue’: not do as you promised (Chinn); no close equivalent is found in OED; it suggests a mishearing of ‘renege’ when playing cards.

‘Ferk’: cigarette; not found in Wright or OED; may be a variant of ‘fag’.

‘Firkle’: (Chinn) to mess about; not found in Wright or OED; firk is a ME verb meaning to move briskly, play a fiddle etc.

‘Fittle’: food, victuals; the OED records this as a rare Worcs variation in 1847; Wright gives it in Stf. War. Wor. Shr. Hrf. Glo. Dor. ‘Fickle’, in the sense of food; is not found in Wright; it may be a mishearing.

‘Fold’, ’fode’: yard or alley; previously fold for animals; this sense of alley or path is reported by Wright in Yks. And Lan.

‘Fourble’: four times (Walker); not in OED.

‘Forby’: nearby, in addition to, with the exception of; Stf., Sc. Irel.; similar to Dutch voorbij; becoming obsolete.

‘Forwhy’: for; widely-used conjunction and interrogative from 1000 to 1500, now obsolete.

‘Frig’: potter; imprecation; used to mean struggle in W.Yks, Ken.

‘Franzy’: a passion, temper; in Stf. and whole Midlands; also framsy in War. recorded 1790.

‘Gab’: loud senseless chatter; general in Eng. Sc. Irel.

‘Gaffer’: foreman, overseer; Yks, Lin. ’Gaffa’ is to laugh noisily, including Stf., though any connection is obscure.

‘Gain’: suitable, sufficient; the opposite is ungain; from Old Norse unreasonable; ‘Gain-hand’ in Yks is convenient; ‘Gainly’ is convenient, good-looking in Yks. also Scots; recorded 1400s and 1800s.

‘Gale’: swinging bar over kitchen grate; Stf. only, according to Wright

‘Gallus’: incorrigible; in Stf.; probably the same as gallows, having the look of the gallows, in Wm., W.Yks etc.

‘Gammy’: lame, feeble; in Stf. Nhb. Yks. Lan. Chs. Dev. etc.

‘Gammittin’: (Chinn) play the fool; Walker gives a practical joke; the OED does not give this spelling; it appears to come from the root game, but could be gambit, gamin, or gamut.

‘Gawby’, ‘gorby’: a simpleton, foolish person; 19th. century; same as ‘gaby’ elsewhere in Eng. Sc. Irel.

‘Gawk’: stare idly or vacantly; in Yks. Lan. Som. War. Glo.

‘Gawp’; not found in any dialect dictionary; may be a variant of gawk; ‘gawpsheet’ is an awkward or ill-kept person in Chs. War; also ‘gaubshite’ in War.

‘Gilliver’: wallflower; derivate of clove-gilliflower, recorded 1225-1400.

‘Ginnel’: entry between two house; northern, esp. Cum. Wm. Yks. Lan.

‘Glaur’: dark; OED gives noun and verb to make muddy; Wright gives mud, scum, also senses of adipose fat and wheedle.

‘Gleeds’: a spark, ember, red-hot coals; in many counties, Sc. Irel.

‘Gog’ as in ‘goose gog’: berry; OED describes it as widespread, starting 1864; Wright does not record it, but has many entries for goose.

‘Goolie’ (Walker): clanger; this needs attestation; OED gives testicles; the nearest sense in Wright is a short knife.

‘Groaty’: a pudding; made of groats; in Sh.I, War.; the basic sense of groat is a coin.

‘Gubbins’: mixture, in Suf. Dev.; iron ore in Shr.

‘Guff’: nonsense, blather; OED gives American uses starting 1897; rubbish of any kind, Cor. according to Wright.

‘Awm’: stalk of a plant; same as haulm in other Midland counties, Sc. Irel.
(This and the next seven words are listed here for dictionary search purposes, although /h/ is never pronounced in BCD).

‘Eavy’; the sense of good or nice may come from heavy-cake, which is made with cream and eaten hot.

‘Iding’: a beating; not in Wright; OED records 19th. century usage.

‘Iver-over’: hover, waver, be undecided; in Stf. War. Wor. Shr.

‘Oof it’: walk; in War. Lei. Lan.

‘Ooter’: nose; OED records post-WWII uses; nearest senses in Wright are steam whistle and owl; the sense of a bowl for heating beer is recorded in Wor. Oxf.

‘Owsomever’: however; found in Shakespeare; Wright records in Sc. Irel. and several Eng. counties, but not Stf.

‘Ump’: ill humour; this sense in Lakel., Bnff. S.Wor. ‘Umpshire’ was the area where men had curved backs from stooped work.

‘Ike’: toss with the horns, beckon with head; same as hike, hoick.

‘Ines’ (Walker): lazy woman; not in Wright or OED.

‘Inkling’: faint or half-concealed desire or inclination; widely used in dialect in Eng. and Sc.

‘Iteridan’: a trivial occasion; only in S.Stf. see Pinnock, 1895; same as aitredan

‘Jack squealer’: the swift; the jack is the comb of a bird.

‘Jack bannock’: a minnow; having a crest; in general use.

‘Jallop’: an enema; Scottish.

‘Jammy’: sense of lucky not found in Wright. OED gives 1850 and Kipling entries.

‘Jessie, ‘Jesse’: a cowardly or effeminate man; a female proper name, probably Scottish usage; not in Wright.

‘Jiffy’: a brief moment; general in Eng. Sc. Irel.

‘Jed’, ‘Ged’: dead; phonetic variation in Stf. Chs. Der. Lei. War. Shr.

‘Jower’, also chower: to mutter, grumble; in Som. Shr. Dev.; onomatopoeic, according to OED.

‘Joe Soap’: stupid person; recorded in OED without etymology; not in Wright.

‘Joey’: a fourpenny bit; this sense was general Eng.; also a narrowboat.

‘Jorum’: a pitcher or its contents; possibly nauseous; a drinking bowl; Walker gives the meaning banquet; may be from jeroboam, or biblical Joram.

‘Jummock’, ‘jummuck’, ‘jimmuck’: shake or jolt; Wright records in S. Wor.

‘Kalied’: drunk; not in Wright; may be from a kalium, a drink containing potassium salts, or a children’s dip.

‘Kecks’: trousers; keck has 10 senses in Wright, including part of cart, flinch, vomit; a possible etymology is the dried hollow stalks of a plant.

‘Keck-handed’; also cack, cag: left-handed, clumsy; in Chs. Shr. Hrf. Oxf. etc.

‘Keffel’, ‘keffle’: a horse; an old or lumbering beast or person; Wor. W.Yks. War.; it is suggestive of French ‘cheval’.. but is more likely to come from Welsh ‘cefyll’.”

‘Kell’: lining around a faggot, according to Walker; in Wright it is caul, the membrane enveloping the foetus; recorded in S. Irel, N.Eng, but not Stf., Wor.

‘Kench’: to bend down, to strain or sprain; not in OED, but recorded by Wright in Cum. Lan. Chs. Stf.

‘Kerfuffle’: fuss, domestic row; originally Scots curfuffle, now general; quite recent, not in Wright; OED gives various spellings after 1946.

‘Kibbles’: small lumps of nutty coal according to Walker; Wright has other senses bucket, strong stick, grinding cereal etc.

‘Kibosh’, ‘Kaibosh’, ‘to put the kibosh on’: to end, put a stop to; possibly Yiddish or Irish; mess, according to Walker.

‘Kiddle’: dribble, as a child cutting teeth; Wor. Chs. Shr.

‘Kind’: thriving, in good condition; S.Wor, Stf. W.Yks

‘Kite off’: to run away; the nearest sense is to fly like a kite, recorded in Lin.

‘Knapper’, ‘Napper’: head; the main sense is flint-knapping, but a knapper head in Wright is a very stupid person in S.Chs. Lin.

‘Knivy’: careful to the point of meanness; Stf. Only.

‘Knock on the ‘ead’: kill terminate; keep quiet according to Walker; Wright records killing unwanted kittens in Kent. Lin.

‘Knocker’: a spirit or goblin that lives in mines; Wright records this in Cor.

‘Knockler’: a tumbler of ale, according to Walker; no such sense is found in OED, nor in Wright

‘Lamp’: verb to beat or thrash; hence lampin’, a beating; main sense is to take long heavy steps; S.Stf. War.; may be an alteration of lam, or to hunt with a lamp; a later sense is a noun for eyes.

‘Lade-gorn’, ‘Lade-gawn’: a wooden pail with a long handle; S.Wor. Chs. Lakel. Cum. N.Yks.

‘Larrup’: to thrash, or beat soundly; in Eng. Sc. Aus.; the other sense of drunk may literally mean beaten.

‘Lezzer’, ‘Leasowes’: pasture, field; Stf. Shr.; found in Wyclif (1388); OED records leasow as pasture, probably from the verb let, and therefore meaning untilled.

'Licker': something astounding; surpassing all others in W.Yks.; feed for a scribbling machine in Stf,Yks. Lan.

'Lief': (Chinn) as soon as; willingly; beloved in Old High German, where is it used as an adverb after the auxiliary verb have, to mean to do gladly.

'Lommock'(Chinn), 'Lummox': large and clumsy; the OED records these meanings, but gives no etymology.

'Loose': to let go, free, to leave off work, to be dismissed; this transitive sense is unusual in standard English; a dialect sense is not recorded in Walker, Chinn, or BBC; leese, meaning to set free is found in Frisian, Dutch, German.

'Mardy': frowning; from 'mar', to spoil damage, interfere with; to spoil a child. Sc. Irel. Stf. etc.

'Maergrum': pulling a face; this spelling, also mergrum, not found in Wright; maigre would be thin, megrim would be headache.

'Maetre' (BBC): friend; this spelling not found in Wright; 'mate' is way of addressing a stranger; maitre would be master.

'Maunch': (Chinn) chew over carefully; probably the same as munch, perhaps from middle French maunger.

'Miffed': disgruntled; from noun 'miff', a slight quarrel; in general dialect use in Sc. Eng. Amer.

'Miskin': ash hill or dung heap; South West Midlands variant of midden, mixen.

'Mither': perplex, muffle, smother, encumber; in Lin. Nhp.; variant of moider; has been claimed as both Welsh and Irish.

'Modlums': breast-feeding, according to BBC web-site, not found in Walker, or Wright; this needs attestation, as no close spelling can be found in OED.

'Moil': work on a dirty job; English regional form, often in phrase toil and moil; from old French *moiler,* to become wet, c.1050.

'Monty': pert (Walker); this is known to informants, but there is no close approximation in OED; mountee would be the ascending flight of a falcon, monte (mountain) the stack in a card game, and manty (manteau) a gown.

'Mooch': to idle or loaf to see what one can pick up on the sly; also play truant; general in Sc. Engl. Aus.

'Mucker': to be in or create mess, to clean out stables; the sense of mucker as friend seems to be British military, probably related to the verb muck in; 'Muckery' in Wor. Shr. is damp or muggy weather; the sense of 'friend' is not explicit in Wright.

'Muggins', 'Mug': a fool or simpleton in War. etc.; now usually referring to oneself; the sense of a person who is easily tricked is found from 1762, though etymology is uncertain; it is not found in Wright; muggins is a call in cribbage to claim points the opponent has overlooked.

'Mumchance': bored, dismal; mum is a dice game, found in Dutch *mommekans*, in 16th. century, played in a mask and silence; hence in extended sense a slim chance, and to keep a dogged silence.

'Nairum': none; possibly from ne'er a one.

'Napper': head; well-recorded, but origin unknown; see knapper above.

'Nash' (Walker): soft; no such spelling is recorded by OED; it may be the same as 'Nesh', soft; this is cognate with early modern Dutch, West Flemish *nesch*, *nisch* soft (of eggs), damp, sodden, foolish (16th cent.).

'Nesh': wet weather; delicate in health; soft to the touch; brittle; in general dialect use in Sc. Eng. Amer.

'Nerker': a mischievous boy; probably the same as 'nerk', a deprecatory term.

'Netty': an outside lavatory; this is described as north-east dialect by OED.

'Nig-nog': fool, novice; this seems to be the same as ning-nong, first recorded in 1832.

'Nincumpoop': a fool or empty-head; written 'Ninkumpoop' in Wor., also 'Nawnypump'; various other spellings in Eng. Sc.

'Nisgul', 'Nisgal' the smallest pig in a litter; smallest of brood of poultry; the spelling 'Nizgul' is not found in Wright.

'Nosh': food; this was a snack or delicacy when recorded in America in 1873, but has come to mean a hearty meal in Britain.

'Orts': leavings; the sense of scraps of fodder left by cattle is recorded in a Latin text in 1325.

'Piece'(written 'pairse' to show phonetics): a part or portion; a slice of bread and butter; mainly Scottish, also War. Wor.

'Paste', also 'Past': to beat, thrash, strike on the face; in Midl. War. Lon. Aust; hence 'pasting', a beating.

'Pie-eyed': drunk; this is U.S. slang, first recorded in 1904.

'Pleck': piece of waste land; the sense of a plot or patch of land is recorded from 1379; it is now mainly known as an area of Walsall.

'Poke': a stye on the eyelid; various meanings around sack, wallet; to swell up, as tumour; sheep jaw disease (Sc.); small-pox; scurf.

‘Ponce’: to sponge; its precise sense is to live off the earnings of a prostitute, but it is also used as a general deprecation, including the contrary senses of a homosexual and an effeminate man.

‘Porket’: a little pig; it has the same meaning as porker, which is in more general use.

‘Potch’: forestall, spite, take another’s place; no such spelling is recorded in the OED, so it may a phonetic variant of poach.

‘Prat’, ‘Pratt’: a good for nothing person; prat meant buttock, in criminal slang (cant), recorded in 1567.

‘Puddled’: stagnant water; prepared clay; tipple W.Yrks, Bnff; this is probably the root of the meaning drunk.

‘Raddle’: blood, red ochre; generally attested as to coarsely colour a sheep; also rouge on a woman.

‘Rantan’: violent mood; ran-tan as a bout of drinking is recorded in Dickens (1853); randan is riotous behaviour, a spree.

‘Raumed’, ‘Raught’, ‘Rawm’: reached; to strain while reaching; the spelling ‘Ream’ with the sense of ‘stretch after’ is recorded in *Ancr. R.* (1225) “Holde euerich his owene mester, & nout ne reame oðres”.

‘Reisty’: phonetic variation of ‘Reisty’ and ‘Reasy’; rancid, esp. bacon; also rusty, discoloured, foul; general in Eng.

‘Reek’: roar with laughter; Walker alone lists this; not in Chinn; the general sense is to emit smoke or smell, but no sense of laughter is found in the OED.

‘Reeves’: strings of onions; recorded in Sampson (1678) “All distended with liquor, and ty'd, like a reeve of onions altogether”; later (1854-96) it is restricted to Northampt., Leic., Warw.

‘Rile’: scramble about; probably phonetic variant of ‘Roil’, meaning roam, wander; attested in this sense from 1400; move vigorously is a dialect meaning from 1788; Chinn believes it is from Old French roeler.

‘Riffy’: dirty; probably ‘reefy’; ‘Reef’ has sense of skin eruption, mange; hence reefy, itching in War Wor. Glo. etc.

‘Rippet’ (Walker): stomach; this needs to be attested; there are no senses close to this in the OED; with this spelling it means tumult.

‘Risles’: peas or beansticks; no OED entries are found for any vowel between these consonants.

‘Robble’: tool used in puddling iron; the OED defines the spelling ‘Rabble’ as an iron bar sharply bent at the end, used for stirring and skimming molten metal in puddling; also, a steam-pipe used for the same purpose.

‘Ronk’: horrible, according to the BBC web-site; with this spelling it is recorded in Sneyd-Kynnersley (1908); it is likely to be a phonetic variation of ‘rank’, meaning rancid, strong-smelling, strong; in War. Wor. meant too strong, also smoky.

‘Rucus’: uproar, disturbance; also spelt ‘Ruckus’ and ‘Rookus’; it is recorded in America in the nineteenth century; it is not found in Wright.

‘Sad’: bread that will not rise; ‘Sad shop’: bread shop; it can also means dense or heavy, which is the probable origin of this sentence from Glasse’s Cookery (1747-96) “It makes the crust sad, and is a great hazard of the pie running”.

‘Saided’, ‘Saded’ (Chinn): contented, full-up or tired; the basic ME sense is sated, while in Wyclif it means constant.

‘Saft’: phonetic variation of ‘soft’ in Stf., also Sc. foolishness, weakness, being easily moved; 'softness’ is weakness of character in Lin. Yrks.; the saft spelling is only found in Scottish literature in the OED; in OE séfte was more usual than sófte or sóft.

‘Sawny’: simpleton; it is recorded from 1700 with this sense, and may be the same as ‘Zany’; the best-attested meaning of zany is a Scotsman.

‘Scribblin-finch / lark/ schoolmaster’: yellowhammer; hurried writing; scribbling also means wool carding.

‘Scrinch’ (Walker): a little bit; etymology obscure; the closest etymologies are a miner's dialect word scrin, meaning fissure, and the verb scrinch, meaning huddle.

‘Scurf’; a variation of scruff (of the neck), found in Yrks., Wor.

‘Scuff’: to box the ears; this narrow sense is not recorded, but may be a particular use of brush lightly; the words cuff, scruff, and scurf seem to be mixed, according to the OED.

‘Segs’: callouses on hands; a segg is ON for callous, but the OED records this sense as late as 1865; the BMJ records ‘planker's segs’ in 1902; also bulrushes.

‘Shilly-shally’: dither, vacillate; originally ‘shill I, shall I’.

‘Shirty’, ‘shaerty’: ill-tempered; etymology is not given by the OED, which records this sense in the 19th. century; the sense of upset is not found in Wright.

‘Shommock’: to walk with a shuffle; ‘Shommacks’: heavy feet or boots; phonetic variation of 'Shammocks', from verb shamble, first recorded 1702.

‘Shut of’, ‘shut on’: free from unwanted attention; the OED says OE scyttan, prehistoric skuttjan would normally be to shit; down to the 16th C. this was the prevailing form; ‘Get shot on’ appears to have become general from the West Midlands.

‘Skinny’: mean, disagreeable; in Stf. Wor. and other Midl. counties.

'Skivvy': a menial female servant; first recorded by OED in 1902, and not found in Wright; the verb 'skive' means shave wood or leather; a skiver, one who splits leather, was widely used in Walsall.

'Skrobble': a tangle; this may be a phonetic variant of scrabble or scribble, to write random characters.

'Slate': criticise severely; a military sense around 1840 was to defeat an enemy; criticism of an author was recorded around the same time; this has the sense of drive off, set on a dog in some Midl. Counties, though not Wor. Stf.; there are various phrases involving school slates; 'Slert' is probably a phonetic variant.

'Sock': liquid manure; the drainage of a dunghill, is recorded in dialects after 1790.

'Sozzled': drunk; sozzle means to mix up liquids; OED says slang in 1890s, with the verb sozzle as a back-formation from this; not in Wright.

'Spangle': a fighting cock; the OED describes this as a fowl or pigeon belonging to a variety distinguished by speckled plumage, first in 1854.

'Spottle': splash; OED records this in Midlands dialects only, first in 1847.

'Spout': the sense of pawn is recorded as slang after 1811; also has senses cry out; talk volubly.

'Spug': house sparrow in War. Wor.; the general English spelling is 'sprug'; 'spugger', 'spujerk' are variants; another sense, of chewing gum is presumably more recent.

'Summat': something; this is the Stf. version, one of numerous spellings.

'Shed': to part, separate esp. sheep; to strike off a piece; general in Sc. and Eng. recorded c.1000 onwards.

'Steen': stone jar; OED gives 'Stean', a vessel for liquids (or, in later use, for bread, meat, fish, etc.), usually made of clay, with two handles or ears; a jar, pitcher, pot, urn, now only dial. and arch.

'Stroddlin': ungainly; this is probably straddling, with -o- vowel; walking with the legs wide apart.

'Suck': lollipop, sweet stuff; in War. Lei. the basic sense is of sucking mother's milk, but also strong drink; OED gives 'sock' as a dialect variant, though this is not widespread in West Midlands, despite the -o-.

'Suf', 'Sough': drain, sewer; subterranean drain to carry off the water in a mine; Latin sub-fundere to flow under; recorded 1440 onwards.

'Swilk', 'Swilker': spill; overflow; or splash; OED records this first in 1674.

'Sye': to pass through a sieve; same word in Old English; OED records this c725 "Seoh þurh claþ", and in Wyclif c1380, "Blynde leders, syynge þe gnatte and swoloweþe camel".

'Tacky bonk': 'tack' is anything of inferior quality; foolish talking; War. Wor.; a coal support; 'bonk' is the o- variant of bank.

'Tansel': thrash; probably from tan, to cure leather, and metaphor "I will tan your hide"; late OE. tannian, c 1000; the -sel is not recorded in OED.

'Ta-ra a bit': good-bye; probably an alteration of ta-ta in Midlands and North; not in Wright.

'Tarradiddle': old wives' tale (Walker); OED gives empty or pretentious talk in post WWII usage, but occurs in a dictionary of slang by Grose in 1796; diddle is to swindle, but tara is obscure.

'Tat': cheap or worthless item; this sense is post WWII; 19th. century sense was a rag; OE tættec a rag.

'Tenter hooks': a state of anxiety; metaphor from main sense of bent nails set in a close row along the upper and lower bar of a tenter, by which the edges of the cloth are firmly held, first recorded 1480, according to OED.

'Thrape': use harshly, abuse, beat; OED gives 'threap' as persist obstinately, to urge or press, rebuke, struggle, etc.; OE. þréapian to rebuke; thrape in Hrf. is to kill small birds.

'Tod': on one's own; this is only recorded by OED after WWII; it may originate from the person playing the role of fox in the game of tod and the lambs; other possibilities are a stump, and variation of "God!" for expressing surprise.

'Towellin': to beat or thrash, in general colloquial use; one sense of the noun towel is to cudgel.

'Ticker': affectionate term for child; etymology obscure; had obsolete sense of a dot or pimple; also single sheaf of barley.

'Tiddler': a hand-reared lamb in Wor. Shr. etc. a small trout in Sc.; 'tiddle' was urinate in War., used by children.

'Traipse': walk in untidy way; OED gives a 1593 entry, and Swift 1710; not in Wright; used widely, e.g. America.

'Tranklements', 'trankliment': trinket, knick-knack, useless article in Yks Chs. Shr.; not in OED.

'Trussen': (Chinn) to trust; OED gives usual meaning of tie in bundles; it may be a variant of the verb truce; the –en might be the Anglo Saxon suffix.

'Tundish': brewer's funnel; OED gives first entry in 1393; not in Wright.

'Wallop': thrash in Eng. Sc. Irel. Amer; written 'whallop' in Stf., Yks; also move fast and carelessly; boil violently.

‘Wammel’: animal; Walker says it is hwaemelec in Old English; alternatively, its form suggests this a phonetic variation, like ‘wum’ for home.

‘Weasand’, ‘Wazzin’: gullet, throat, windpipe; this is in Worcs. spelling; numerous other spellings in Sc. Irel.

‘Wench’ : girl, woman; formerly widespread in English, persists in this area with non-derogatory sense.

‘Werrit’ ‘Worrit’: to tease or worry; as noun a cause of worry.

‘Whut?’, ‘Oot’: this could be the Oxfordshire phonetic variant of ‘woot’, a call to a draught animal to veer to the right; not in OED.

‘Yampy’: deranged; the nearest sense to deranged in Wright is yamp, meaning noisy; the verb yammer means to cry out noisily.

References

Ancrene Wisse. The library of Virginia University has a searchable corpus of Middle English texts at (Nov 2006) www.lib.rochester.edu/camelot/teams/awintro.htm

Asprey, Esther (2003). *Language and identity in the Black Country*. Cambridge Linguistic Conference 2003: 303-309.

Baker, Peter (2003) Introduction to Old English. Oxford: Blackwell. Online version at www.wmich.edu/medieval/research/rawl/IOE/pometer.html

BBC local radio Black Country www.bbc.co.uk/blackcountry/voices2005/index.shtml

Bibby, Bob (2001). *Grey paes and bacon*. Bridgnorth: TravellersEye Books.

Cheshire, Jenny (1998). English negation from an interactional perspective. In Trudgill,P. and Cheshire,J. *The sociolinguistics reader*. London: Arnold.

Clark, John, and Yallop, Colin (1995). *An introduction to phonetics and phonology, 2nd. Edition*. Oxford: Blackwell.

Chinn, Carl and Thorne, Steve (2002). *Proper Brummie: a dictionary of Birmingham words and phrases*. 2nd. edition. Studley, Warks.: Brewin Books.

Chinn, Carl (2004). *Black country memories*. Studley: Brewin Books.

Dieth, Eugen and Orton, Harold (1951). *A questionnaire for a linguistic atlas of England.* Leeds: Leeds philosophical and literary society Ltd.

Ekwall, Eilert (1936). *The concise Oxford dictionary of English place names.* Oxford: Clarendon Press.

Fletcher, Kate (1979). *The old testament in the dialect of the Black Country*. Parts one and two. Pub. The Black Country Society, 49 Victoria Road, Tipton, West Midlands; now at P.O. Box 71, Kingswinford, West Midlands, DY6-9YN.

Gelling, Margaret (1992) *The West Midlands in the Early Middle Ages*. Leicester: Leicester University Press.

Heath, Christopher (1980) *The pronunciation of English in Cannock, Staffordshire*. Pub for the Philological Society, Oxford: Basil Blackwell.

Hogg, Richard (ed). *The Cambridge history of the English language, Volume 1.* Cambridge: University Press.

Hogg, Richard (2004). The spread of negative contraction in early English. In *Studies in the History of the English Language II: unfolding conversations*, edited by A. Curzan and K. Emmons. Berlin: Mouton de Gruyter.

International Phonetic Association (2003). *Handbook of the International Phonetic Association: a guide to the use of the International Phonetic Alphabet.* Cambridge University Press.

Jenkins, Alf (1982). *Titterstone Clee Hills: everyday life, industrial history, and dialect.* Published by Alf Jenkins, Bower House, Orleton, Salop, SY8-4HR.

Jespersen, Otto. (1946). *Modern English grammar on historical principles, Vol. 5.* London: George Allen and Unwin.

Jordan, Richard (1974). *Handbook of middle English grammar : phonology.* Translation of Handbuch der mittelenglischen Grammatik Lautlehreand revised by Eugene Joseph Crook. The Hague: Mouton.

Kuhn, S.M. (1990). *The Vespasian Psalter.* Ann Arbor: University of Michigan Press.

Ladefoged, Peter and Maddieson, Ian. (1996). *The sounds of the world's languages.* London: Blackwell.

Langland,W. (1380). *Piers Plowman.* http://etext.lib.virginia.edu/ .

Laghamon (1205). *Brut.* http://etext.lib.virginia.edu/ (where it is spelled Layamon)

Mathisen, Anne Grethe (1999). Sandwell, West Midlands: ambiguous perspectives on gender patterns and models of change. In Foulkes and Docherty (eds.) *Urban voices.* London: Arnold.

Mulcaster, Richard (1582). *Elementarie.* Electronic version at the University of Michigan www.hti.umich.edu/cgi/p/pd-modeng/pd-modeng-

Orton, Harold, Sanderson, Stewart, and Widdowson, John (1978). *The linguistic atlas of England.* London: Croom Helm.

Orton, Harold and Dieth, Eugen (1962) *Survey of English dialects. Vol. 2: basic material. Parts 1-3: West Midlands counties.* University of Leeds

Oxford English Dictionary Online. Subscription service via www.athens.ac.uk.

Roper, John (1968). *Wills of Dudley: 1601-1650.* One copy of the mimeograph at Coseley library archive, another at Lichfield. The original handwritten wills are at Lichfield record office.

Rowlands, Marie (1987) *The West Midlands from AD 1000 (Regional history of England).* Harlow, Essex: Longman.

Saussure, Ferdinand (c.1916). His linguistics lectures were published only posthumously. Some of his principles may be found on the wikipaedia web-site.

Smith, Jeremy (1999) *Essentials of early English.* London: Routledge.

Stratmann,F.H. (1974). *A Middle-English dictionary.* Oxford: The Clarendon Press.

Sweet, Henry (1882). *Anglo-Saxon Primer*. Revised by Norman Davis (1952) Oxford University Press.

Tolkien, JRR and Gordon, EV (Eds) 1967. *Sir Gawain and the Green Knight.* Oxford University Press.

Trudgill, Peter (1974). *The social differentiation of English in Norwich*. Cambridge: University Press.

Walker, Ted. (undated). *The definitive Black country dictionary*. Published: E. Walker, 50 Walsall Street, Wednesbury, West Midlands, WS10-9HA.

Wells, John (1982). *Accents of English, vols I – III*. Cambridge: University Press.

Wright, Joe (ed) (1898-1905). *English dialect dictionary: being the complete vocabulary of all dialect words still in use, or known to have been in use during the last two hundred years, founded on the publications of the English dialect society and on a large amount of material never before printed.* Vols. 1 – 6. London: H.Frowde.

Index